THE SMARTERCHARTER MONOHULL GUIDE: CARIBBEAN

Insiders' tips for confident Bareboat cruising

DAVID BLACKLOCK
MICHAEL DOMICAN

Illustrated by
KIM DOWNING

After Irma and Maria

UNLUCKY STRIKES

What Happens Now?

Hurricanes are a fact of life in the Caribbean. Just as the monsoons batter Asia every year and cyclones create havoc in the Pacific, hurricanes hammer the islands of the Caribbean and the Atlantic and the coast lines of Central America and the continental US—and sometimes even end up in Europe.

They come every year, and every year the islands get buffeted. Some islands just get grazed, others take a horrendous beating. Some, like poor Haiti and its neighbor, Cuba, get run down year after year. Islands that are above the magic 12° 40′ N parallel of latitude are all susceptible to the hurricanes' rough embrace, those below largely exempt.

Some years the most powerful storms rage impotently, touching land nowhere and disappearing from public memory. In other years, individual hurricanes seem to bounce from one island to the next wreaking extraordinary havoc as they go. Almost every island in the Caribbean has its own story of desolation and destruction. But still the residents persist, rebuilding and picking up the pieces. As will happen this year, too. It's home. It's what you do.

As we write this, the 185 MPH winds of *Irma* and *Maria* have destroyed much of the infrastructure of the biggest sailing centers of the Caribbean. The British Virgin Islands, St. Martin, Dominica, the US Virgin Islands and Puerto Rico are torn asunder. But within a few weeks, a few months, the green shoots will poke out and regrowth will commence. As we have seen in the Virgin Islands already, new growth is decorating the hills just a month or two after the storms' passage. But it won't be like it was before. At least not right away.

Or, to be more exact, it will be like it was before—twenty years before.

Where there have been fine restaurants and themed bars there will be the old original—people on a beach with a cooler full of beers and fish on the grill. There will be a generator for the blender —and for the music. For many sailors, that is the preferred mode. The sailing will be as fine as ever, the sailors probably finer, in that the feeling of camaraderie will be strong. There will be guitars. There will be dancing on the beach.

If that seems daunting, bear in mind there are dozens of destinations in the Atlantic and Caribbean without any of the complications we've described. From the Bahamas to Grenada there are islands aplenty, each with its own charms, its own language and history. Maybe now's the time to pull out the charts and take a look at what's out there. The major charter companies have bases in many of these locations: *The Moorings* and its sibling, *Sunsail*, have bases in Antigua, St. Lucia, Grenada, St. Vincent, and Canouan and have just announced a new Exuma base in the Bahamas. *Horizon Yacht Charters* are also in Antigua, Grenada and St. Vincent. *Dream Yacht Charters* are in Guadeloupe, Martinique, St. Vincent, and Grenada—as well as Cuba.

And there are plenty of local operators with boats on the dock in these and other locations ready to welcome you aboard. So, if you had been thinking of going to the Caribbean this year, hold on to that thought. Get in touch with your preferred charter companies and ask for their suggestions.

DEPENDING ON CREW EXPERIENCE AND, YES, *CONFIDENCE*, THERE may be more options than you had thought.

Sailors have told us again and again that every year or two they feel the tug of the islands. "I need the Caribbean," they tell us. Well, right now the islands need them, need us.

It may be a little complicated finding the right charter at the right time but the effort will be worth it. And you'll be taking part in the revitalization of people and place that, without timely intervention, may not quickly flourish to their full potential.

In the words of the immortal *Captain Ron*: "If it's going to happen, it's going to happen out there." Let's go. Let's make it happen.

Introduction

Chartering a yacht in an unfamiliar location is not much different from renting a car in a foreign country. You know how to drive and you know how to read a map—in fact you have a trusty electronic assistant to help with that part. But it's the other traffic, the unfamiliar signs, the roundabouts, and the overpasses that give you pause.

Do I turn left or right here? Is that a good place to park? What does that sign mean? The *gas-oil*, is that diesel or petrol? *Oops*, I mean gas—or do I? As with driving abroad, it's the first day or two that are the most challenging—even when coping with driving on the opposite side of the road, or with a confusing signage system. But by the end of a week you're charging down the Autobahn like you were born to it.

You can read all the books, study up on the regions, talk to friends who have done it before, but once you step aboard a 40-foot-plus yacht crewed by your family or friends in often breezy conditions—well, things can seem a bit daunting. Especially when the weather forecast is in an unfamiliar language or dialect, delivered via a crackling radio.

We're here to help. We've spent years sailing the Caribbean and know that our experience could be of benefit. We aim to share our knowledge and a few tricks we've picked up about the region and its inhabitants—and to have you confidently sailing a modern yacht around some of the most beautiful and accessible cruising grounds the world has to offer.

Now, bareboating Caribbean style doesn't have to mean sloppy sailing with a *Red Stripe* in one hand while you steer with a sunburnt foot. Rather, it means confidently sailing a well-appointed yacht in close-to-ideal conditions without the issues that often plague higher latitude sailors—unpredictable weather, chilly temperatures, foul weather gear, fog, big tidal ranges, and strong currents—or windless days better suited to water skiing than sailing. At least not all the time.

Yachts in the world's charter fleets have become rather sophisticated in recent years. They boast greater sail area and more intricate systems. Many now sport generators, air conditioning, and a wi-fi connection. Some larger models might even power a watermaker.

This sophistication brings with it a greater convenience but it can also bring greater complication and confusion. Electrical systems can always misbehave, generators can quit in the middle of the night. Murphy's great law prevails: If it can, it will. (Break down, that is). But fortunately, along with the sophistication of the sailing yachts there has been a related improvement in customer service—help is but a (free) phone call away.

Sailing is an art. There's a science to it, of course. But there is rarely just one correct way to do anything on a boat, bareboat or otherwise.

Whether it be docking, anchoring, sailing upwind or down, tacking or jibing, there is almost always more than one way of pulling it off.

So, if you have a technique that works and that won't break or scratch anything—or raise your blood pressure (or that of anyone around you)—stay with it. But we hope our guide will add to your body of knowledge and perhaps offer a fresh perspective on some of the familiar aspects of the sailor's skill set.

Research and planning are the keys to any successful voyage. An excellent source for information on the Caribbean is the message board Traveltalkonline.com. If you're new to the area you wish to charter, go on this site a few weeks or months prior and ask questions—you'll get some excellent information from fellow sailors or visitors.

Another good source is Noonsite.com, which has extensive information on the cruising grounds of the Caribbean—and the rest of the world, too. In addition, many of the specific islands have related Facebook groups for cruisers and sailors which are worth exploring.

Also recommended is freecruisingguides.com which is a great source for, well, free cruising guides, as well as hosting the Caribbean Security Index, a useful tool for reporting and assessing risk in and around the area.

A NOTE FOR READERS OF THE PRINT EDITION

As there are a number of links to material mentioned in the various chapters, we have removed most of the links from the pages themselves and placed them on a dedicated page at the web site: https://wp.me/P9jJzL-53

Perhaps the simplest way to access these links would be to have an internet capable device close to hand whilst reading. The links are arranged by chapter and page number, so should be easy to locate.

NOTE: *The individual charter company web sites have a wealth of informa-*

tion for the destinations they serve. By scanning them all you can get a compre-hensive idea of the options and attractions available throughout the Caribbean.

'

Chapter 1

SOME BACKGROUND

The Caribbean Charter Business

The charter yacht trade has many homes—Greece and the Aegean, the Mediterranean, the Adriatic, Thailand, Mauritius, Fiji, Tahiti, The Great Barrier Reef, The Bay of Islands, Baja California, the Pacific Northwest and many more.

But nowhere is there such a variety of available boats coupled with ease of access as the Caribbean. Just a few hours' flight-time from the US and Canada, with Peru, Chile, Argentina, and Brazil within a comparable radius of distance, there are thousands of modern yachts in comfortable anchorages in countries with familiar facilities and modern supermarkets, more or less. Flights from Europe make non-stop journeys to Antigua, Martinique, Guadeloupe, Puerto Rico, St. Lucia, St Martin, the Virgin Islands and other points.

THE COUNTRIES AND TERRITORIES OF THE CARIBBEAN ARE generally relaxed when it comes to the certification and qualifications of skippers and crew. Unlike Europe, where 21 countries request an International Certificate of Competence, the authorities of the Caribbean have few specific requirements. The charter companies themselves, of course, do—as well as requiring an in-depth resume and often a checkout sail with an in-house professional, who has authority to suggest you take a skipper with you.

Some companies are stricter than others—a trait that favors the consumer in that the stricter companies tend to have the less-abused and better-maintained boats. Most require a comprehensive sailing resume for the designated skipper and, on larger boats, at least one other member of the party.

The main differences among the charter grounds of the Caribbean lie in the convenience of travel, ease of shopping, and the distances that have to be covered when getting from one anchorage to the other. It's no surprise that the busiest charter grounds in the region—the British Virgin Islands—are a short distance from mainland USA, deal in US dollars as their official currency, speak English and are very stable politically. Not only that, they are laid out in such a way that a chain of small islands on the south-eastern edge provides protection from waves from that quarter, while the larger islands provide a great degree of shelter from the storm-generated swells emanating off the North Atlantic. The resulting relative calm in the main channel of the chain, the Sir Francis Drake Channel, explains its colloquial name, *Drake Lake*.

RECENT DEVELOPMENTS ANNOUNCED BY MAJOR CHARTER companies suggest new cruising grounds, from Cuba to Grenada, are opening up. Currently, Dream Yacht Charters offers a base in Cuba and another in Puerto Rico. Others, such as The Moorings, Sunsail, Horizon and more are branching out there and elsewhere.

Airports are being expanded, too, as islands compete more fiercely for the tourist and leisure traveler. And even without airport construction and expansion, new participants continue to join the market. Currently there are direct flights from New York/Newark, Miami and other US and Canadian cities to over a dozen sailing destinations all over the Caribbean.

EAST FROM THE BVI, THE CRUISING GROUNDS OF ST. MARTIN LIE exposed to the swells rolling in from the North Atlantic and Africa. Farther south, the Grenadines and other islands present some challenges in the distances a boat has to sail to get from one anchorage to another—though those difficulties are offset by the relative lack of other cruisers, making these islands almost at times a private playground.

Where sailors begin their Caribbean chartering career is purely a matter of choice and convenience. Many cruisers began chartering in the soft waters of the BVI before venturing further down the Antilles chain. The options available will suit every preference—some destinations have direct flights from Europe and the US, some are a bit harder to reach—while the sailing becomes a little more challenging. As you venture east and south, the sailor is obliged to fend for himself to a greater degree—which is not necessarily a bad thing.

MOST OF THE CHARTER COMPANIES CITED ABOVE HAVE BASES further down the islands. St. Vincent, Grenada, Guadeloupe, Martinique, Antigua and Barbuda, St Martin and its neighboring islands—as well as those destinations already mentioned—are well served by the major companies and some local ones as well. These destinations are, in the main, well served by air transport, too—either directly or with one stop along the way. There is room for the sailor who wants to charter a boat for day sails whilst staying overnight in a villa by the beach as well as the family looking to cover some ocean miles.

We know a family from Germany who came regularly for over a decade and sailed from the BVI to Grenada and then island-hopped all the way back up to Tortola again. This 6-week odyssey filled their souls and gave them memories to cherish for a lifetime—or at least to hold them until they could come back two years later. They stopped only when the kids' new careers kept them from coming.

The Caribbean is a sailor's playground, able to indulge all manner of bareboating adventurers with options fitting every level of expertise and experience.

So when choosing a charter company it pays to learn whether they offer discounts for future charters and other inducements, loyalty programs and the like. You can also negotiate for better prices at different times—or if no shift on the pricing, the company might offer you an extra day or a night's pre-boarding or a free kayak. It's always worth trying, though the newest boats are usually in solid demand and not subject to discount. Ask where the best deals might be—maybe one of the other islands is doing less business than projected and is priced accordingly.

On the other hand, it might be in your interest to pay a little extra to cement a relationship with a top charter company. As competition increases, incentives will surely follow—and loyalty rewarded.

A yacht is an expensive asset to own. Anyone who lives near a marina will have noticed that boats seem to sit in their slips for most of the year—going nowhere and doing nothing. As yacht ownership has diminished over the past decade or more, the yacht charter business has increased exponentially. Why own a yacht when you can rent one for a week or two in different parts of the world? Or, why not own a yacht that allows you to sail a similar model in different parts of the world whilst yours is earning you an income?

This change in boating habits has been one of the drivers behind the rapid innovations in yacht construction and design—which in turn have made the charter yacht the attractive option it has become.

BUT WHILE CHANGES ARE INEVITABLE, THE CHARTER BUSINESS IS and should long remain a strong pillar of local economies. Each year the boats get more comfortable, the amenities more varied, access more efficient, destinations more welcoming. The great secret of yacht charter is that it has many price points from the top tier to the relatively inexpensive, but once you're on the water the fun is the same and the experience, well, priceless.

We look forward to seeing you out there!

Chapter 2

PREP TALK

BEFORE THE CHARTER

When we first discussed this book, we brainstormed on the subject of who our ideal reader might be. The person we imagined was one who had some experience as a sailor and had taken lessons, perhaps gained a certification or two. They had been on a charter before, either with a professional captain or as a member of a group charter with someone else skippering the boat. Maybe they even owned a boat themselves. Perhaps they had skippered their own charter with family and friends aboard—but had found it less than relaxing. There was so much to do, so many things to consider, no one to help with the tedious but necessary tasks that go into running a boat.

Along with this somewhat experienced sailor, we also believe that a cruising couple or group who operate their own boat and anticipate covering many miles as part of a circumnavigation or a year(s)-long sabbatical cruise might benefit from our experience as well.

Whichever profile sounds familiar we know where you are coming from, since we all started in the same place. No one is born a sailor. Some people have great advantages of course—as with all things in life—but those advantages are no guarantees of aptitude or ability. We learned everything we could, we asked questions, we read, we listened, and we persevered. Mostly, though, we got in a boat and went sailing.

SAILING IS VERY MUCH A MENTAL PROCESS—WE CONSTANTLY monitor invisible forces such as winds, tides, and currents. And we have to adjust physical objects to harness those forces—sails, salty lines, recalcitrant mechanicals, and sensitive electronics.

When sailing with a crew, we need to organize and co-ordinate their actions—and prepare them for the expected requirements of the day.

Much of this involves research—tides, weather—as well as chart work and close reading of the cruising guides. And now there is so much information available to us right on our phone or tablet that we often can get the facts we need in real time.

BEFORE COMING ON CHARTER, THERE ARE SOME ESSENTIAL TASKS that need to be tackled. This is a great opportunity to develop crew cohesion. The Head Honcho, aka Skipper, can ask different members of the party to do research, to practice techniques, to get themselves into the adventure mindset. If you are partial to Facebook, Instagram, or other social media platforms, you could set up a private group for all participants. Or just a simple email group will suffice. That way people can share photos, web sites, articles, instructional videos and other relevant information.

Crew Assignments:

Here are some assignments you might consider:

- First and foremost—practice your knots! The #1 most-neglected aspect of boat operation is the mastery of these basic knots—the Reef Knot/Square Knot, Bowline, Clove Hitch, Cleat Hitch, Round Turn and Two Half Hitches, Figure 8/Stopper Knot, Sheet Bend, Cow Hitch, and Rolling Hitch. Consider having a knot-tying session on Day One of the charter to make sure everyone has the same idea. It's a safety issue—you want to be able to rely upon your fellow sailors to be able to secure a knot without too much hesitation. See link information at the end of the book.

- Create simple Passage Plans for each day's sailing (with options for those days when you decide to do nothing but loll on the beach or snorkel the reefs). These can be done way ahead of time and can be multiple choice. That is, make rudimentary passage plans for each day given an easterly wind, a westerly wind, no wind, too much wind etc. Also, be modest about your daily mileage. A trip of 20 miles can be a 5-7 hour sail. Your companions might not want to be that long on the water, at least at first. The key to a good day's sail is an early departure! See link information at the end of the book.

- Compose menus for the daily meals. Put together a spreadsheet for each day's requirements and base your shopping on it. See link information at the end of the book.

- Assign positions to your crew based on their expertise and experience—helmsman, trimmer, navigator—and let them do their research. Younger crew can perform wonders as lookouts, fender monitors, toy wranglers and the like.

- Suggest reading material for your crew—guidebooks, charts, online discussion boards.

Gather Information:

- E-mail the charter company to confirm what items are included on the boat and what are optional extras—toys (such as Stand Up Paddleboards), floating toys, Wi-Fi, safety netting (for young children), hammocks and the like.
- Also ask the charter company for provisioning information, such as which companies deliver to the boat. Look on the online discussion groups, such as Traveltalkonline.com, for references and preferences.
- Request an inventory list for such items as towels, soap/shampoos and galley cleaning gear, garbage bags and insect spray. Some charter operators provide a 'starter pack' to cover you for the first couple of days, others don't provide anything in that department at all.
- Often the charter operator provides a cruising guide on the boat. But it's a good idea to have a copy ahead of time to help with your planning. It's a great way to keep a record of your trip, too. You can ask the charter company if they'll send you a copy (some do) or else get one from Bluewater Books (bluewaterweb.com), Amazon, or your local bookstore.
- Explore options for rendezvous dives or lessons, eco-tours and other high-demand frolics. Be cautious about making commitments far in advance, since weather and other factors might dictate last-minute itinerary changes that make it difficult to keep appointments. You can most often book a dive or other activity when you arrive for your charter—or the week prior to your leaving—and are better able to make an informed decision on weather and itinerary.
- Browse web sites to see what events might be upcoming at your destination—Full Moon parties, national holidays, Mardi Gras, Carnival, New Year's. French

islands have their special days, as do the Dutch, British and US territories.

Personal Assignments:

- Consider your clothing options: people often bring far too much. T-shirts (or equivalent), shorts, and sandals or flip-flops are the general rule though you might want to dress a bit for a night out. You can always bolster your supply of beachwear at many of the bars, restaurants, and boutiques along the way. One complication is that if you leave home in winter, you'll need warm clothing for your beginning and ending segments—which you may be able to leave at the charter base rather than bring onboard.
- Bring rash guards and swimming tops (for stingy thingies), snorkels and masks that fit properly (kid-sized ones particularly) though the boat will come equipped with a variety of sizes. If you are chartering in the winter season, prepare for some (relatively) chilly evenings. Bring a fleece-type jacket or similar. And everyone should have a wide-brimmed hat with a lanyard for sun protection.
- Luggage is a sensitive issue. Storage is at a minimum aboard the boat though you might be able to store empty bags—or ones stuffed with your winter gear—at the charter base while you are on the water. Soft luggage like a duffel bag is preferred for the boat since it can be rolled up and stowed under the bunk. Also, the farther afield you go—and the more flights you have to take—the more likely that a bag could go missing, so pack as lightly as possible.
- Check with your doctor for all your medications—you may need to renew prescriptions.

Bring medications in their original containers and bring copies of all prescriptions, since authorities have been known to request them.

- Ask for seasickness remedies. Scopolamine trans-dermal patches are highly effective but not for everyone.
- Make sure all documents are up to date—passports, driving licenses etc. Do you need visas? Let your credit card company know your plans—even if they say you don't have to, do it anyway since the Caribbean is a bit of a trigger for the banks. They may send a text or a phone call that you are unable to access requesting a response before they release funds.
- See if your phone plan includes the country you'll be in —otherwise roaming will suck up money.

Gear to Bring:

- Hand-held VHF radio. If you have one, bring it—with charger. Not every bareboat has a working radio at the helm location, so it's not always easy to talk to dock staff when operating the vessel. Plus you can carry it ashore and communicate with the mothership when it's time to be picked up by dinghy.
- Hand-held GPS, with spare batteries or charger, likewise. For when the main chart plotter goes down (in an electrical storm for instance). You may not need it—but when you do, you really do. Many mobile devices have a GPS capability—but make sure yours can work independently of Internet hookup.
- Some short (10 foot) length of thin but strong (*Paracord*, but ideally Spectra, which is less stretchy) line. Your bareboat won't have many spare short lengths of strong line, which in handy for a multitude of jobs from lashing

the steering wheel to securing the dinghy fuel tank to keeping the Stand Up Paddleboard (SUP) attached to the boat. Leave it behind when you finish charter. And before leaving the charter base, take a walk around the sail loft or riggers' shed and see if there are some bits of line lying about. The guys are usually pretty relaxed about your taking a bit of old rope. Ask first!

- LED headlamp for BBQ operation, night-time anchor inspection (with a red-light option), dinghy operation, and a host of other uses, such as reading in the cockpit at night.
- Pack your own basic first-aid kit with anti-bacterial cream, your preferred pain relievers, sun cream (SPF 30 is sufficient), top-level sticking plasters (Band-Aid type), and any other favorite brands. Most places in the Caribbean carry US brands along with French, Dutch, and British—depending on where you are.
- Bring plenty of multi-sized zip-lock style bags. They are good for bagging sunscreen, toothpaste, and other messy stuff as well as wet stuff such as bathing suits; and documents, electronics and other sensitive items
- A good underwater camera is always useful—you'll kick yourself if you don't bring one.
- Hammock (the netting type, without crossbars) plus attaching straps to rig between mast and forestay or (on a cat) transversely across the stern area. Some smaller ones can be rigged in the cockpit area for storing fruit such as oranges and bananas and/or dive masks etc.
- Insulated drinking water bottles.
- *Sharpie*-style marker pens and masking tape to mark items such as water bottles, can and bottle tops for quick identification in a fridge or cooler. Also bring white electrical tape (*not* masking tape) to mark running rigging such as the main halyard, reefing lines etc.
- *Speedo*-type swim goggles for use when operating the boat during rain squalls. Ski goggles (mask-type) will work

even better. These are good because the nose is free—unlike with a dive mask where the nose is encapsulated in the body of the mask and creates fog.
- Mini flashlights.
- Dry Bag: if you want to go ashore by paddle board—or swim to that famous bar that won't let you dinghy over.

Money Matters:

- Bring plenty of cash. Many of the islands have inefficient communications, even at the best of times—making credit card payments unreliable. Phone connections can go down, internet traffic can be awfully slow. In addition, many banks charge extra for the Caribbean, making it expensive for the business owner, so they insist on a high minimum amount for credit card charges or impose a fee for the service. Cash is king. In many places the US dollar is easily accepted, even in Euro areas.

NOTE: Access all links at https://wp.me/P9jJzL-53

WHAT TO BRING (Personal Items)
All the following must fit into a single soft duffel-type bag.

First question: Shoes/ no shoes?

ANSWER: IT DEPENDS. MANY SAILORS PREFER TO GO BAREFOOT on the boat. Which is fine until you stub a toe on a deck fitting or slip on a wet cabin sole. If you do choose to wear shoes onboard, they must have a light-colored sole. White is good. They needn't be fancy $100 nautical jobs—grab a $20 pair from the Big Box store or the supermarket. They only need to last a week—leave them behind for the dock guys. Never wear them off the boat—they'll just bring sand and dirt aboard. A slip-on type rather than a lace-up is best. So long as they have a decent grip they'll do. Off the boat you'll be wearing flip-flops. If you prefer to wear shoes, bring a second pair for shore-side.

2-3 pairs of decent shorts

1 pair of long pants

1 T-shirt per day (buy any extras at the bars and restaurants as you sail by)

2 shirts (with long sleeves preferably. *Columbia*-style fishing shirts are good)

1 dress shirt with collar

6 pair underpants (you won't need to wash them, and they take up no space. Pack them up in a plastic bag and take them home)

2 swim suits

1 sweater or vest (for cool evenings)

1 waterproof jacket

At least one pair polarized sunglasses (plus safety/retainer cord)

1 good protective hat

sunscreen + moisturizer

toothbrush, shampoo and the like

Medications (bring a copy of any prescriptions)

Plus any favorite teas, music, books, games etc.

NOTE: If you are taking multiple flights, bring a carry-on bag with a change of clothes, swim suit, and toiletry items etc. for a couple of days. The more changes you make en route the greater the likelihood your luggage will not arrive at the same time as you.

Chapter 3

LOGISTICS

PRE-ORDER PROVISIONS

No matter which island destination you choose, or which charter company, your arrival at the charter base can often turn into a confusion of conflicting priorities and last-minute adjustments. Not only will you be exhausted from the preparation and the travel, but there will be briefings to attend, supplies to purchase and stow, crew to instruct—amongst other things. One time-saver is to ask your charter company about pre-ordering provisions. Many of the islands have supermarkets or specialist vendors that offer this service—or the charter company might do it in-house.

ALTHOUGH IT MIGHT SEEM TEMPTING TO SIMPLY PRE-ORDER everything and have it available when you arrive—

what happens if your flight is delayed or your boat isn't ready—do you really want your steaks, seafood, and dairy items sitting in the hot sun for hours?

Hold off on the perishables, but do order your packaged, canned, and bottled items—especially water. Get the heavy stuff dropped off, leaving you free to shop around for meat, seafood, fruit, vegetables, cheeses, and other delicate items. Your charter company should be able to provide links to local stores that'll deliver direct to your boat. And most larger islands can accommodate diets of the gluten-free or vegan variety these days.

It helps to have a good idea of what you'll need for the duration of the trip. Charter chef Deb Mahan gave us these tips:

- Create a basic spreadsheet with a menu plan for each day. Working from that, you can be precise about the amount of vegetables, starches, and proteins that you will need. Count how many chicken breasts, how many rashers of bacon, the number of eggs and so on.
- As storage space is limited and refrigeration not always reliable, it's best to plan to eat the more perishable items earlier in the charter.
- Start your shopping list with items required for the first meal of the day through to dinners. As you think of an item, group it into *proteins, fruit and vegetables, dry goods,* and *grocery items.* You can then pick out non-perishable items that you can pre-order ahead of arrival, making your personal shopping much easier.
- The fewer spices and condiments, the better. Storage is restricted and quantities required are small. Pack some favorites at home and stick them in your luggage.
- Plan your itinerary to include a stop with a supermarket or decent grocery halfway through your trip.
- Have a meal ashore at a recommended restaurant every second day or so to give the chefs a break—and to make the provisions last a bit longer.
- There's a link to a basic Meal Plan spreadsheet at the end of the book.

And ask about genuine local producers for a taste of fresh

locally grown fruit and vegetables. In several Caribbean islands there are farmers and purveyors of indigenous fruit and veg. We have assembled a number of links to purveyors and provisioning stores throughout the Caribbean. Access all these links via https://wp.me/P9jJzL-53

CONSIDER BRINGING SPECIAL FOODS SUCH AS FROZEN MEATS OR seafood with you, packed in dry ice or just stacked while frozen inside a good travel cooler, such as a Yeti. Check with your airline!

Water toys and other items such as Stand Up Paddleboards (SUPs), kayaks, noodles, even an extra dinghy can be ordered through your charter company and their partners. A second dinghy makes potential conflicts more manageable when the kids want to do one thing, the dads another, the ladies something else.

NOTE: *All the web addresses and telephone numbers were correct at the time of publication, but we advise you to confirm data.*

Chapter 4

CREW CONTROL

KIDS ON BOARD

Not every sailing vessel is ideal for young children, so extra care must be taken. Monohulls may heel over alarmingly on occasion, leaving the little ones sliding about. Narrow cockpits and constant clambering up and down the companionway make them less than, well, companionable. If you have small children on board, ask the charter company to add netting around the perimeter of the boat. Most will do so for a small extra fee—but the cost is nothing compared to the peace of mind it can induce.

Regardless of age, you must have lifejackets that fit your children. Ask ahead of your arrival and check that they are aboard when you get there. If you have some at home that the kids are familiar with, bring them along if you can.

Do the same with dive masks: if the kids have one at home, pack it in the luggage—that way they won't have to endure an oversized leaky mask. At high season, choice may be restricted at the charter base. If your kids are small, bring small swim fins too, if you have them at home. These are items that not all charter companies are able to provide—though they might have partners who can supply them to you if needed.

MANY OLDER KIDS (OVER 10, SAY) LIKE TO GET INVOLVED IN THE operation of the boat. There are many things they can do—sort out swim fins and masks, check that SUPs and kayaks are firmly attached to the lifelines, monitor the dinghy if it's being towed, and even operate it if they fit the criteria laid down by the charter company. They can even sweep out the saloon and help with garbage and other tasks that are essential every day such as clearing laundry off the lifelines prior to setting sail. Have the older kids be responsible for checking bilges, emptying holding tanks and generally making themselves useful. In return, they might like to steer the boat for a while. And they make great lookouts!

If there are younger kids—under 5—plan for short passages for the first day or two.

Sailing can get boring for young kids on long days. Books, jigsaw puzzles, board games, and the usual digital toys will be welcome.

Girl makes friends with gulls.

Kids love to learn new stuff. BVI charter captain and instructor, Donna Smith Acquaro says, " I recommend encouraging children to learn along the way. Bring books with the flora and fauna of the area. Also, drawing materials and shock- and water-proof cameras."

And look at what your charter company (or local third-party vendor) offers in the way of water toys. These are age-dependent but range from swim noodles to kayaks and SUPs. Also take a look at your local drugstore or mall outlets—they often have kid-sized inflatable toys and the like at ridiculous prices. Many folks bring these toys and leave them on the boat when they're done.

Parents often bemoan the fact that kids on a boat seem to want to spend time texting on their phones or watching *Harry Potter* on an iPad, rather than enjoying the gorgeous azure waters. But we have found that it pays to indulge the young set initially. The boat is an unfamiliar environment—often much friendlier to adult preferences than to youthful ones. In a day or two the kids ought to relax and adapt. If not, it's easy to distract them with trips ashore. In most island destinations there are often stops along the way with kid-friendly food and sand beneath the feet.

A little family hiking trip can change the atmosphere immediately. Some restaurants offer kid-friendly entertainment, such as pirate shows and sing-alongs and for older kids there are surf clinics and kiteboard lessons. Ask at your orientation/chart briefing if there are any child-oriented shore stops.

Some island beaches feature amenities such as inflatable climbing walls, safe and easy snorkeling areas, even sandpits and playpens—*aka* the beach. Older kids (parents too) might enjoy hiking to the top of the island on dedicated trails to take in the view. Some areas feature horse and pony riding and other activities to suit various ages.

If all else fails, you'll at least have the onboard Wi-Fi to conjure up some silly videos—just don't check the news.

Chapter 5

ADULT EDUCATION

THE CHART BRIEFING

This briefing is an essential element of the bareboat charter. While it is very rarely brief and it's not merely about the chart, it is crucial that the skipper and at least one other crew member attend. If time permits, and the crew are interested, bring them all.

Most charter companies offer a group briefing for all outgoing charters, either in the early evening the day prior to charter or the morning of the start day—sometimes both. You'll learn about the area and the environment in detail, as well as current events both cultural and meteorological, so be sure to take notes for later reference.

This is an important resource even if you've sailed in the area before—things change all the time and memory is not a reliable navigational instrument! If some of your crew arrive late, have them sit in on the next available briefing. That way you'll all be on the same page.

If you hope to get out of the base quickly, the remaining crew could be going through the ship's inventory, stowing provisions, doing any last-minute shopping or sorting swim fins, topping off water tanks and all the other sundry tasks that remain undone. The following are among the topics covered in the chart briefing—and be sure to ask if something you are concerned about isn't specifically addressed:

- How to get a local weather forecast and where to get updates via VHF or local radio each morning or evening.
- Swell warnings and projected weather events.
- Any recent biohazards that have been reported (jellyfish during summer months, fly outbreaks, Sargassum seaweed beachings).
- Local dos and don'ts—dress codes, for instance.
- Current events that can impact your trip—some islands have powerboat Poker Runs at various times of the year. These might affect your ability to anchor or find a mooring at a favored destination on a particular day. And they often take over the fuel docks for hours, so you aren't able to replenish diesel and water. Also there are various Full Moon parties and such that may require finding a mooring much earlier in the day than normal.
- A sample itinerary with the most popular stops described —as well as the No-Go areas, where your insurance coverage might be void.
- Recommended itineraries
- Communications protocols, such as phone numbers for assistance etc.
- Procedures to follow on return from charter such as refueling requirements.
- Areas where you're likely to be approached closely by a photographer in a dinghy taking pictures…she may even be flying a drone over you!
- Local crime warnings such as dinghy theft hot spots.
- This is the time to clarify the types of Navigational Markers you'll encounter, such as Cardinal Buoys, and

any special rules, off-limit areas etc. At various times of the year, often in the winter/spring season, there are sailing club flotillas and other groups that, while fun to share a dance floor with ashore, can make finding a mooring somewhat challenging. Such groups won't be all leaving from the same charter base as you of course, so ask around. We often ask the provisioning staff at the biggest supermarkets if there are any large groups they're supplying and which company they're chartering with.

- Try to obtain an itinerary from any such flotilla—just walk up to one of the participating boats on your dock (you'll know by the flags and banners flying from the topping lift) and ask. Customer Service personnel at the charter company should have an itinerary sheet at their disposal, too. Then you can sail off in the opposite direction—unless you'd rather follow along! Some areas are host to regattas put on by the sailing magazines such as *Cruising World* or *Sail*. *The Yacht Week* is a gathering of young college-age sailors from around the world and can be boisterous. So check when you are booking your trip whether there are any such expected.

- You can also ask the personnel on a crewed yacht if they know any information that could assist you. Usually they are only too happy to advise—they'd rather help out before you start the charter than have to help out when boats drag anchor at midnight in an unruly and crowded anchorage!

- Be sure to take a record of any relevant phone numbers for things like medical clinics, emergency services, hospitals and the like. The information you get from the Chart Briefing can impact the writing of your Passage Plan. This is an outline of the day's projected course and heading and destination, with hazards highlighted and waypoints described.

- You may have written your passage plans weeks before

you arrive in the islands. If not, research tide heights and times, phases of the moon, particular events at different destinations. You can write up a number of alternate plans and, depending on the weather patterns on the day of charter, you can choose which one to implement.

Chapter 6

HANDS ON

THE BOAT BRIEFING

Even for the most experienced sailors, the Boat Briefing is the one piece of instruction you don't want to miss before leaving the safety of the charter base. Charter company staff will lead you through the on-board equipment and operational procedures of the vessel. There is a lot of information to absorb—one way to deal with it is to delegate aspects to different crew members. Have one person—someone with knowledge of the subject—specialize in the engine operation, another in anchoring systems etc.

Bear in mind that the briefers have a sequence to follow. One piece of information leads to another, so try to hold your questions until the briefer gets to that topic—once items get out of sequence, things can get skipped over or missed entirely. But don't hold back— if you are not confident you understand an item, ask for more information and make notes as you go. Some of the most frequent questions concern the following:

Autopilot: An invaluable item so long as you master its operation. Make sure that all crew learn the procedures, too. It's not unheard of for a helmsman to inadvertently hit the "Engage/Auto" button and find he can no longer steer the boat—

and not be sure why. Check that the Autopilot is disengaged when you depart the dock, otherwise you might T-bone the boat across the way. When motoring long distances, the autopilot is often the preferred helmsman, but it must be monitored. Ask whether your autopilot allows for *Course* or *Wind* settings and how to access these.

Mark the center point of the steering wheel with some electrical tape. Rotate the wheel from hard a-port to hard a-starboard and halve the number of turns. Place tape at Top Dead Center. Cross-check with the autopilot display.

Battery Charging: Make sure you get proper instruction in battery-charging procedures when running engines for that purpose. Before leaving the dock, disconnect the shore power cables and observe the change (if any) from a charging voltage to a resting, or true state. If there is a substantial difference, you may have problems with your batteries.

A fully charged 12-volt battery system should be taken to a level of 14.2-14.4 volts initially, if there is no drain on the system. Once the charger is disconnected, the voltage should fall to around 12.8 volts. Don't let it get any lower than 12 volts

—and even that is too low a charge, about 25% of capacity. Ask how to properly monitor battery states of charge. Learn how to properly disengage the transmission (into neutral) when charging at higher rpm—and make sure any operating the vessel understands this, too. It's not unusual to see boats flying around in circles while still attached to a mooring ball when the transmission slips into gear while the engines are in charging mode. Sometimes this happens when no crew are aboard.

Bilge pumps: Make a basic map of their locations. Particularly ask to hear them in action. Get all aboard to become familiar with the sound of an active bilge pump. It might indicate a leaking water tank, or it might simply be a stuck float switch—one that needs to be poked with a broom handle or boat hook to reset—so know how many float switches there are and their locations.

Boat papers: If you are planning on going to another jurisdiction—crossing from the BVI to the USVI or St. Martin to St. Barts, for example—make sure you have the requisite papers. The charter company needs to know beforehand if you're planning such a trip, since it may affect the choice of vessel they supply to you—some individual boats may not fit the regulatory requirements. Request customs forms, too. You'll need the boat's registration information and, when returning to the original port of departure you'll need a copy of your cruising permit. These are usually located in the chart table. Make sure there's a chart in there as well. And remember that when clearing in to a new port you'll need your clearance from the previous one. Read the fine print closely, since some forms require many signatures, as well as addresses and other details for all passengers.

Chart Plotter: Second only to the depth sounder, the most important piece of equipment in the cockpit is the chart plotter/GPS. Take the time to understand the proper sequence for loading pages, entering information and saving waypoints and routes etc. Are the depths in feet or meters? How to engage/disengage alarms? Ask the briefer to locate the instruction manual for the equipment. Often it is buried under a seat cushion in the saloon somewhere. If you can't locate it, go online using the boat's wi-fi and download a copy from the manufacturer's web site.

Cockpit lockers: Go through them thoroughly, since this is where you'll find emergency equipment, flares, PFDs etc. Also swim fins, masks, dive flag, and other useful gear. You may be able to organize lockers so as to stow some beverages and other bulky items.

Depth gauge: Is it calibrated to read from the sea surface, from the transducer (about 1-2 feet below the surface), or from the bottom of the keel? Whichever it is, make sure you know how to calculate your true safe depth for operation. And if it's in meters and you'd prefer it in feet (or vice versa) ask your briefer to change it for you.

Dinghy security: On a monohull, learn how to properly

attach the lifting bridle. If you're on a catamaran, learn how to secure the dinghy in its davits to prevent it swinging side-to-side when hoist. Ask the briefer to supply a length of light line for this if not already provided and to locate and demonstrate the security cable and lock for the dinghy. Get into the habit of locking the dinghy to the mothership every night.

Emergency tiller: Where is the emergency tiller and how does it fit to the rudder stock? Ask the briefer to demonstrate how to use the cockpit winches to turn the tiller when the boat is underway (when water is flowing over the rudder, you won't be able to do so without some mechanical assistance). It may sound extreme but boats lose their rudders more often than you'd think by hitting a coral head, a rock, or floating debris. The latter is more common in the summer when tropical storms dump torrents of rain on the steep hillsides, washing fence posts and other hazards into the waters.

Engine operation: Go over everything from the correct starting procedure, to the fuel system, to emergency stop procedures. Some boats will have a key start but most now have electronic starts that require a sequence of switching. Make sure you understand it, since it's easy to turn off the ignition whilst the engine is still running—possibly damaging the alternator. See where the fuel refill port is located (we know a group of bareboaters who pumped the bilges full of diesel after mistaking the emergency tiller cap in the cockpit sole for the fuel intake).

NOTE: A good estimate of fuel consumption is around 1 gal/4 liters per hour for every 40HP/28Kw. Your generator would be about half that rate at full load.

Entertainment tech: Boats come with a variety of entertainment options from big-screen TV to multi-stage audio players with inputs for direct connectors, Bluetooth, and other technologies. In some cases you'll be able to direct cast from your tablet or phone direct to a big screen or sound system, so ask for a full explanation. If you have a teenager onboard, they might be the best option for gaining rapid insight into the complexities of the system.

First Aid kit: The kit supplied with the boat does not always have the best selection of treatment options. Someone is going to need it at some point since an insect bite, a stubbed toe, sunburn, even a jelly fish sting (or a hangover) are not outside the realms of possibility. Make sure it is fully stocked and have available the additions you brought with you—high quality Band-Aid type plasters, antihistamines, good pain relievers etc. Keep the kit in an easily accessible place and make sure everyone knows where it is.

Freshwater pump: You will go through a tank of water per day, even more. The Universal Water Rule is

---

"Fresh water lasts in inverse proportion to the amount of hair on the boat."

So, if you have a group of teenage girls aboard, be warned !

IF YOU HAVE MORE THAN ONE WATER TANK (NOT ALL BOATS DO), you'll have to switch the manifold valve from one tank to the next. Have everyone become familiar with the sound of the running water pump—it could mean either a leak, a tap left running, or it might indicate that the water tank is empty and the valve needs switching. It is often hard to hear the pump when the generator is running. The water pump can often run "dry" but only for a short period—repeated dry runs day after day may burn out the pump. If the boat has a watermaker, you'll run it for at least a couple of hours every day. Get a thorough instruction in the intricacies of this equipment. **Avoid having all the water-tank valves open at the same time**, since the higher tanks can bleed down into the still-full lower tanks, putting immense pressure on the seams—sometimes leading to a breach in the side of that tank and the loss of your potable water.

Generator operation: Master how properly to start and stop it. Locate the reset button in case the generator quits—usually because of being overloaded—and won't produce any current after restarting. There is generally a push-button reset on a bulkhead panel next to the generator. Also become familiar with the instruments on the saloon breaker panel. Locate the through-hull that feeds cooling water through the generator. You'll need to know which is the dedicated seacock/through-hull for the cooling water intake. This intake is of a narrow gauge and is is liable to be blocked if there is much free-floating Sargasso-type seaweed around (generally in the summer), so learn how best to clear it.

Inventory: There should be an inventory list or manifest aboard the boat. Go through this thoroughly with the briefer. For two reasons: 1) because you'll be charged for items not on the boat when you return and, 2) most important, it's the best way of learning where everything is.

Propeller and rudder(s): Find out if you've got right or left-handed props, a Sail Drive or fixed shaft. Check your rudder type— some monohulls have twin rudders, for instance—and location. Also —should the propeller be allowed to rotate freely when under sail or should you engage reverse gear to stop it from spinning?

Check your boat's prop walk tendencies by engaging slow reverse while securely tied to the dock—first making sure that your spring lines have no slack in them—and look over both sides of the boat forward of the cockpit to see which side the prop wash appears. If you see the stream of turbulent water on your starboard side, you have a right-handed prop and your stern is kicking to port —or would be, if you weren't attached to the dock. If the stream is directed to the port side, you have an unusual left-handed prop— and your transmission turns in a counter-clockwise direction of course—while your stern kicks to starboard.

Reefing lines: There should be at least two reefs pre-set in the main. Follow the lines aft and check the colors of the lines tied around the boom (reef #1 is always furthest aft) and follow them forward to verify that they are correctly labeled at their clutches.

Refrigeration: Check the location of the thermostat and that it is properly set. Some boat refrigerators get very cold and can freeze lettuces and other fragile vegetables—not to mention eggs and milk—so learn where the cold plate is. Make it a routine to move items around or place a barrier of a small sheet of cardboard (from, say, a wine box) or bubble wrap to prevent items from touching the plate.

Running rigging: Sort through the lines that run through blocks and sheaves. These lines are often color-coded, so ask for an explanation if you are uncertain. This category includes mainsheet, jib sheets, halyards, reefing lines, downhauls and outhauls—any moving lines.

Stack Pack: (The canvas cradle holding the mainsail). If it has a zipper along its top, unzip it before leaving the dock—and don't bother with it again until the end of your charter. If you have an in-mast furling mainsail, request a demonstration on how best to reef and furl it.

Stove operation/Barbecue grill: Few things will drive you crazier than a stove that won't light or won't stay lit. Many stoves and ovens are self-lighting but we recommend you buy a long-barreled stove lighter—one that can reach all the way to the back of the oven. These units vary from boat to boat. Make sure you get a thorough training in how to light it and how to control temperature. By "thorough" we mean have the briefer actually light it—not just point at the controls and give a verbal run-through. This is temperamental equipment—but crucial to the wellbeing of skipper and crew! The BBQ might be either gas or charcoal. If the latter, get the pre-treated type, with lighter fluid already applied. If it's blowing outside, we sometimes start a few lumps indoors by lighting them in a frying pan then (carefully!) take them outside to the grill and build up our coals there. Though check your charter contract, since some forbid having lit charcoal inside the vessel.

Toilets and holding tanks: The marine toilet is the most important piece of equipment on the vessel. Pay close attention to the briefing, since a malfunction can have serious consequences. Most monohulls have at least one toilet available for general use—so if one toilet goes down, the crew will still have access to a public unit, usually accessed from the saloon. Locate the holding-tank outlet valves. You will be using them pretty much every day, so either make sure the occupants of the relevant cabins learn how to work them, or delegate the task to a single person or on a rotating roster. Before leaving the dock, check all toilets to see that they are flushing correctly and are free of blockages.

VHF Radio: Learn how to operate the unit and, if close to US territories, how to get a weather forecast by accessing the WX button. A surprising number of VHF units are set to the wrong channels or seem unable to receive signals. Make sure yours actually works properly by performing a radio check with the dockmaster prior to leaving the charter base, or by using your handheld unit. Know how to make a Mayday call. And make sure as many crew as possible get this briefing since, in a real emergency, some could be incapacitated or busy on other tasks.

Windlass and anchor: Learn how to release the clutch by letting it freewheel for quicker anchor dropping. And make sure the release handle for the clutch is always close to hand in case of emergency. If you've brought some colored cable ties with you, attach them at regular lengths, beginning at 20 feet and every 20 feet after. Locate the anchor snubber line and ask how to attach the hook.

Anchor ball: Locate it and learn how to assemble and raise it in the boat's fore-triangle. Ask how best to secure the main halyard to stop it from wrapping around a spreader or slapping against the mast. Have the briefer supply you with a length of light line to secure it, if not already provided.

Chapter 7

DARK SECRETS

HEAD MASTERY

Traditionally it's The Heads, or The Head, but let's be bold and call it the toilet. It's the most important piece of equipment on the boat and is as sensitive as an opera star. Treat it like it's #1 and it won't behave like it's #2, OK?

nothing…NOTHING…goes down the toilet unless it's been down your digestive tract first.

Well, maybe paper. Small pieces of paper. No wads, no fistfuls. Little pieces, a couple of sheets at a time. And flush between the sheets. No toe nail clippings, razors, dental floss, hairclips, rings, tampons, watches, false teeth—you name it, they've all been in there. So please keep all foreign objects out of the bowl. No baby wipes, 'flushable' or not. No hair from the hairbrush. No bits of fluff off your shirt. Nothing but little bits of TP.

The reason is that, on most modern charter yachts, everything that goes into the toilet has to pass through a very small and weak blender/grinder called a macerator. If things get stuck in the macerator it can't do any macerating. You do not want to listen to your toilet attempting to digest a toothbrush. It's no fun. That means someone has to get down on hands and knees and disassemble the whole shebang and clean it out and re-seal it, which often means unscrewing the toilet base from the floor of the bathroom and generally turning the Throne Room into the Poop Deck. Bad!

Many of the new units on larger boats now flush with fresh water but most still use salt water. Except for the need to keep your water tanks topped-up, there is no tangible difference as far as you are concerned, but in the long term the fresh water device is a better proposition—less corrosion, less odor.

NOTE: *You must return to the base at the end of your charter with the valves draining the holding tanks in the OPEN position.*

Almost all the units you will encounter will be electrically filled and flushed via a rocker switch, which supplies fresh water into the bowl and pumps the bowl contents out, through a macerator and into a holding tank. The most common model of toilet also has a separate *rinse* rocker switch, which does what you imagine it does.

THE PROPER WAY TO USE THE TOILET IS, AFTER RAISING THE LID:

- First, pump water into the bowl.
- Then sit down on the open seat. And gentlemen, this includes you. Yes, sit, every time.
- Then do your business, whatever form it might take.
- If necessary, wipe the sensitive parts of your body.
- Carefully flush the soiled sheets, one or two at a time. Baby wipes or paper towels go into the available

receptacle—usually a sealable paper or plastic bag. Save plastic shopping bags for this purpose or bring/buy a box of small plastic bin liners.

- Flush away the evidence.
- If the evidence refuses to completely disappear, flush again. And again. Leave it as you'd like to find it.
- When all evidence has disappeared, press the rinse button and then pump out as much water as possible from the bowl so it doesn't slosh around and spill over the lip of the bowl underway.
- Close the seat lid so that nothing small accidentally falls into it from a nearby shelf while underway.

Flush the bowl empty so there's little to no water in it. Close the seat at all times when not in use—things can fall into the toilet and really jam up the works. That includes baby wipes.

If your boat has a manually operated toilet, pay close attention to the instructions of the boat briefer and, as we have mentioned, ask that they demonstrate *procedures and not merely describe them.*

The Game of Thrones:

Your boat will come equipped with holding tanks that receive and store the black water from the toilets. When you're in bays and harbors – and anywhere people are swimming around the boat— keep those tanks closed by way of shutting the valves that you were shown during your boat briefing. It is important that you empty the tanks on a daily or every-other-day basis. Do it when you are *en route* from one anchorage to the next and as far offshore as you're going to get. It's good to include the evacuation of the holding tanks as part of your daily Passage Plan. And make sure you comply with local regulations regarding discharges—not in National Park areas, for example.

While the valves need to be closed when you next enter an anchorage or marina, it is most important that you return to the base at the end of your charter with the valves draining the holding tanks in the OPEN position. If you return with full tanks, you will likely be assessed a fee.

Chapter 8

CLEARING OUT

GOING CLEAR

The islands of the Caribbean are variously self-governing entities, such as Dominica, or overseas dependencies of large nations, such as the British Virgin Islands or the US Virgin Islands. Some islands share allegiances—such as St. Martin/Sint Maarten. The ABCs (Aruba, Bonaire, Curacao) are affiliated with the Kingdom of the Netherlands and thus the EU. Whenever you leave one jurisdiction and enter another you will be required to file paperwork with either one or both places. Some may require visas, while others require only money.

None of the officers you meet and to whom you'll offer your documents is in any hurry to rush the process along. But don't be tempted to debate any of the requirements or betray too much impatience—you'll only delay the proceedings. You may feel as if your presence deserves some kind of reward—you are bringing your hard-earned money to spend in this little paradise (whatever it's called). But to the officers, you are simply a person to whom they may or may not grant the privilege of entry. It's their paradise, after all. So be polite and patient and ask a few questions about the best places to see. It is often to your advantage to begin every conversation with "Good morning," or "Good afternoon," whichever is appropriate, as the first words of your first sentence. Wait for the reply. Then you could ask something like is there a restaurant featuring the island's food to advantage? Churches are often a fertile topic for conversation—ask if there's one of significance you might visit.

IF YOU DO WISH TO TAKE YOUR BOAT TO A DIFFERENT jurisdiction, check ahead with the charter base. Some companies have restrictions on where you can take their vessels and they may need to supply you with extra paperwork such as the boat's original documentation, import permits, proof of insurance. They'll know what's required and whether or not you need to clear out of the country that you're in before you leave. They may also need to supply you with a boat that can pass the requirements for entry to that jurisdiction.

Most charter companies will have the yellow *Q* flag on board but the courtesy flag for the country that you're visiting may not be included in the yacht's inventory. Check before you leave because not flying the correct courtesy flag (or flying it upside down) is, well, discourteous.

Before you leave the charter base where you'll have access to a photocopier, make multiple copies of your crew manifest—names, addresses, passport number, occupation—as some territories require as many as 3-4 copies and you may be visiting more than one foreign territory. A trip starting in St. Martin, for example, may also include Anguilla and St. Barts—sometimes in the same day.

When you get to where you're going, make sure that your former courtesy flag (or pennant under the starboard spreaders) is down and exchanged for the yellow *Q* flag. In fact, the former should have come down when you entered international waters since you were no longer in territorial waters. If you're just planning on staying a day or two then you can ask to clear in and out at the same time, so as to avoid having to come back and do more paperwork before you leave. Some islands allow you to stay 48 hours this way; some more, some less.

Are the crew permitted to go ashore whilst the captain is clearing in the vessel?

Some island territories are very strict, some are lax and most are reasonable. We're not naming names, but we suggest you check the boat's cruising guide (and websites such as Noonsite) for the list of the ports of entry and the exact location and opening hours of the government buildings you must visit. One important piece of information is whether the crew are permitted to go ashore whilst the captain is clearing in the vessel. Some jurisdictions are very particular on this point.

Also, the time of year is important. If you arrive in, say, St Barths around New Year you will find it filled to the brim with mega- and super-yachts with attendant crew, celebrities, and craziness. This is not the best time to present the Customs and Immigration authorities with difficulties. They are overwhelmed with sensitive issues already. Have all your documents ready, passports open and a smile affixed. And be prepared to wait. Show up six months later, you'll find the harbor empty, the officials relaxed, and you might even get a space right on the dock.

When going ashore, bring a waterproof bag for carrying documents and passports (it might be a wet dinghy ride to clear in). And don't forget a pen! You might need local currency (Euros, EC dollars, US dollars) to pay entry fees. Not everyone takes credit cards.

And after you've cleared in with both Immigration and Customs, and before you wander out to explore the town or have a leisurely lunch, you should send someone back to your boat to take down the 'Q' flag and replace it with the courtesy flag of the country you've now legally entered.

Chapter 9

CHAT

INSTANT MESSAGING

Clear communications aboard the boat are crucially important in creating correct conditions. The conditions being desirable results —a good spot to anchor, a well trimmed sail, an early warning about an upcoming fish trap. This can mean sharing a terminology —does everyone involved in sailing know the names of the parts of the boat and the terms used for describing actions aboard ship? Or it may mean agreeing on a system of signs and signals. Does everyone know how to communicate a danger or an opportunity—a line in the water, an empty mooring ball? How will crew communicate with the helmsman from the far end of the boat?

Clear communications create correct conditions.

When approaching a dock or mooring ball, the helmsman needs to know how far the object is from the vessel and which direction to steer. In close quarters, the best method for conveying this information is by way of hand signals. Verbal communications at a distance of 40 feet are not effective. The observer at the bow is generally upwind of and facing away from the helm—any shouted information will get lost and distorted in the inevitable wind. The helmsman will have no chance of getting his or her commands and questions heard at all.

The best solution is to decide upon some simple, clear and unambiguous signals—which generally go only in one direction, from bow to helm—that will convey information instantly. There are no rules for the type of signal to use—no global standards, no universally agreed gestures (other than the rude ones). There are, though, many intuitive and obvious ones that you will doubtless agree upon. The main thing is to make them in a somewhat exaggerated manner—that way there will be less confusion.

FIRST THERE MUST BE CLEAR, UNOBSTRUCTED SIGHTLINES between bow and helm. The deciding factor on where the bow person should stand is decided by where the driver's controls—engine, instruments and VHF—are located. Port or starboard? Whichever it is, the bow person needs to adjust so they can be seen clearly by the driver—who must be able to view the bowperson clearly as well as the surrounding boats, docks and other hazards. If there are sightline difficulties, you can appoint a person to relay the signals but this is not ideal.

SIGNALS ARE BEST WHEN UNCOMPLICATED, SO PRACTICE THEM IN the cockpit area before implementing them properly. The signal should be maintained for as long as the procedure is needed. With an occasional exception—for instance, keep the fist raised and clenched to signal for neutral, but then extend the arm out to indicate the direction to turn the boat.

Below are the signals we have found work the best:

SHOULD THE BOAT BE IN GEAR OR IN DRIFTING IN NEUTRAL?

- Neutral: Clenched fist raised at ear height.
- Forward: Open vertical palm/*tomahawk chop* in direction of desired movement at ear height. Increase rate of hand movement to reflect desired speed.
- Reverse: gentle pat on the buttocks—*it may sound silly but it works.*

WHICH WAY TO STEER?

- Extend arm and hand in direction boat needs to go — if you're right-handed and need to indicate a turn to the left you'll need to raise your hand above your head and bend your elbow to prevent your body from blocking the driver's view of your arm. Direction to steer in neutral is the steady hand pointing the appropriate way.

DISTANCE OFF DOCKS, NEARBY BOATS AND MOORING BALLS?

- The best way for the driver to judge distance off a dock or other obstruction is to have an observer stand somewhere within—but not blocking—the helmsman's field of view, with arms fully outstretched. Midships might sometimes be better than at the bow.
- Have them wait until the dock comes to the same distance as their fully outstretched arms (let's say that span is 5' 6" / 168 cm) before beginning the procedure. Any distance more than that is not an issue.
- As you approach the dock, your crewmate brings their hands together to indicate the distance-off. This visual representation is clear and precise and can be used when squeezing through a narrow gap in a marina or mooring field—as well as when approaching a mooring ball.

- Start the signal at one or two boat lengths off the target
  —more if there is a lot of traffic or heavy wind affecting
  progress—when approaching a mooring or anchor drop.
- When docking, the first signals may be describing
  direction and speed but may revert to *Distance Off* when
  close to the target. And when docking, the signals person
  may have to communicate direction, speed *and* distance-
  off at the same time!
- This person effectively has control of the boat—so
  sightlines must be clear. When docking, make sure the
  line handlers don't get in the way. At the same time, the
  driver is responsible for overall safety and seamanlike
  decision-making. Right-of-way rules need to be observed
  at all times.

OTHER USES

Often on charter boats, the Bimini and dodger can get in the
way of sightlines when crew are hoisting the mainsail. If you can,
drop the dodger. Hand signals are just as useful as with docking etc.
and can describe both vertical and horizontal action (hoisting and
trimming sails). In this case the signals are informing the winch
grinder when to apply pressure and when to desist.

These are some signals we've found effective.

A single vertically extended finger rolling around from a lightly
clenched fist indicates the following:

- *Grind-on* — when the finger is pointing towards the top
  of the mast (for raising the main)
- *Ease or drop* — when pointing at the deck (for easing or
  dropping the main)
- *Trim-in* — when pointing at the jib sheet (for trimming-
  in the jib)
- *Ease* — when pointing to leeward (for easing the sheet)

IN ALL CASES THE FOLLOWING SIGNALS ARE GENERALLY WELL understood:

a) Palm of hand raised in the universal traffic cop gesture means just that: STOP.

b) Thumb raised in universal OK shape signifying *Okay* or *Good*.

NOTE: SPEND A FEW MOMENTS WITH THE CREW GOING OVER these signals at the beginning of each day—until you're sure they've got it!

Chapter 10

LOCAL KNOWLEDGE

BOAT BOYS

In the Leeward Islands—from the Virgin Islands to Dominica —enterprising local men, known everywhere as *Boat Boys*, offer valuable services. Approaching your boat in mooring fields and anchorages (but not marinas) they will offer to sell you ice, take away garbage and sometimes offer you provisions—local or otherwise.

Before coming alongside they will usually ask if you want what

Boatboys in Bequia offer their services

they have and if you say *"No thanks"* they'll just move on to the next boat. They will not harass you if you don't want what they're selling.

Further down island, in the Windwards, *Boat Boys* can be a little more insistent about the value of their services. There are three common situations:

Mooring Services:

A hail will come from a man

in an open boat who has sped out of the bay and made a beeline to you as you make your approach.

"Welcome to the island, Cap. I got the safest mooring in the bay. Follow me and I'll lead you to it and help you pick it up."

"No thanks, we're planning on anchoring".

"Anchoring not safe here, Cap—bottom is foul with weed"

"But my cruising guide says it's great holding on a sandy bottom!"

"It was, but the weed grow over it now."

Having had the seed of doubt planted in your head and conscious of your need to keep your boat and crew off the rocks, you're now tempted to ask about his safest mooring.

So you follow him in and he takes you to a weed-encrusted old ball and pennant with a dubious-looking downline that you can see through the turquoise waters.

"Are you sure this is safe? It doesn't look it!"

"Yeah, Mon! Haven't lost a boat yet!"

Now, most often these moorings are safe—despite their looks. But you're often better off to anchor on your own ground tackle assuming that the cruising guide rates the holding good and, of course, you're confident of your anchoring skills.

Provisioning: One of the gastronomic pleasures in the Caribbean is the fresh local tropical fruit. No supermarket-bought mango or banana will taste as good as one picked that day at its perfect degree of ripeness. And there are other delights like papaya (paw-paw) and star fruit. In the Windwards, *Boat Boys* will come alongside and ask you to buy from them. If you turn them down (perhaps because you're fully provisioned, or just bought from another vendor) they can sometimes affect disappointment and become indignant. We don't mean to paint them with one brush—we appreciate their services—but we just wish that we didn't have to go through the pantomime so frequently.

Security: When the *Boat Boy* who offered you a mooring said *safest* he sometimes also implies that on his mooring, he'll look out for your boat while you're ashore. If you choose to anchor—well, who knows what may happen? This is intended as less of an implied threat as an extra reason for the newly arrived cruiser to take his ball. He probably wouldn't be looking out for your boat even if you took his ball as he knows that theft on boats in his bay is extremely rare. That said, some bays are prone to crime and your charter company will alert you to those at the chart briefing. You can also look them up as you plan your trip beforehand by checking out these online community sources:

TRAVELTALKONLINE: HTTP://BIT.LY/2GCJKJI
    Noonsite: http://bit.ly/2hGLzlK
    Caribbean Security Index: http://bit.ly/2hxRhU1

AT THE DINGHY DOCK

"I'll watch your dinghy Cap—just EC$5 —no one take it"

Your newish RIB with its shiny outboard engine represents quite a temptation in the more impoverished Windward Islands with their higher levels of poverty and unemployment. So this is one area where we would recommend giving the most sincere-looking boy at the dinghy dock a few $E(astern)C(aribbean) (the rate against the US dollar is nearly 3:1) for the peace of mind and good karma that it'll provide. Be sure to take a friendly photo of the both of you with your dink in the background—just for the memory, of course.

Now, it must be said that—like business folk everywhere—the *Boat Boys* rely on goodwill and the maintenance of their reputation. It's not in their interest to harass, intimidate, or rob their customer base. Word quickly gets around. But some sailors would prefer to not have to deal with them. Some sailors just don't like to be bothered. But if you treat the *Boat Boys* as a resource—the same way they look at you—and ask where to get a taxi or where to find fresh batteries, you might be pleasantly surprised by the response. As citizens of the islands, the *Boat Boys* do feel proprietary about the place —you, after all, are coming to their home. And they do know everything and everyone.

It's surprising how pleased you are to see someone who is offering what you need, when you need it—and how much you look forward to his arrival, even at 7am!

AND EVERYWHERE YOU'LL FIND A NUMBER OF LOCAL KIDS WHO might come to your boat offering ice and a garbage pickup. It's surprising how pleased you are to see someone who is offering what you need, when you need it—and how much you look forward to his arrival, even at 7am! As everywhere, folks are hustling to make a living. A few bucks for a bag of ice makes a big difference to these purveyors, so try to spread some joy where you can.

Chapter 11

TALK RADIO

Smooth Transmission

As the world of electronics grows continually more sophisticated, the gear we see on new boats has grown ever more complex and capable. That trusty standby of marine communication, the VHF radio, now sports many new refinements. Not all of these, however, will be activated on the unit aboard your charter bareboat.

But the VHF will be a constant part of your daily routine, so make sure that the boat briefer instructs you in detail how it works. They come from various manufacturers and each has its power, volume, and squelch controls in different places—so familiarity with one brand may not be helpful when faced with a new one. And be sure to do a radio check before you leave the base.

Have a couple of crew sit in on the VHF briefing—they can pass on the knowledge to the others. It is an essential piece of safety equipment and may be a literal life saver. In addition, it will be in use several times each day for making dock or dinner reservations, hailing dive boats, checking weather forecasts etc.

WHILE WE WOULD GENERALLY ADVISE YOU NOT TO RELY ON YOUR

mobile phone for making emergency calls, some Caribbean jurisdictions—the British Virgin Islands, for one—have emergency services that do not monitor VHF frequencies at all. So if an emergency should arise, use the VHF for an initial call and to monitor responses (with VHF, you may get assistance from a nearby boat, for instance), but also use your phone to call the emergency numbers as provided by the charter company.

In the BVI, Channel 16 calls are monitored by US Coast Guard personnel in the US Virgin Islands and requests for assistance may be routed to local BVI responders. But a phone call to the all-volunteer BVI Search and Rescue (VISAR) will probably have a quicker response. (There is generally a notice stuck to the bulkhead by the navigation station with emergency information for the local sailing area. It will be covered in your briefings as well.)

Instructions for contacting Search and Rescue along with radio protocols.

But it's not only the dire emergency that makes the VHF so useful. One not uncommon occurrence for bareboaters is the loss of a dinghy when the tow line comes undone. This happens most frequently in the early stages of the charter when knot-tying skills are still a bit rusty. Or the towing eye might pull out from the bow of the dinghy. Several times over the years we've seen a dinghy floating downwind with an oblivious crew sailing happily away. No matter how many times we hailed the vessel, we received no response. This can create a situation that is a) costly for the charter crew and b) dangerous, since the dinghy is also the vessel's lifeboat. So, think of the VHF as not only the best way for you to contact the world, but for the world to contact you.

In general though, the VHF is your go-to communications tool. Its defining feature is that it broadcasts to anyone with a working

receiver, whereas phones are one-to-one. This broadcasting capability means that aid is just as likely to be a nearby vessel or shore-
based assistance, as an official search and rescue or emergency
responder. Also, rescue services often are able to create a single line
of position from just a few seconds of listening to your MAYDAY or
other emergency call.

NOTE:

- Become familiar with changing from High to Low power
  —not to save electricity but to take up less VHF
  bandwidth. If the marina is one mile away you don't
  need to broadcast your request (and hog Channel 16) up
  to 20 miles away.
- Learn how to adjust the Squelch control, then leave the
  setting alone during your charter.
- If you own a handheld unit with which you are familiar,
  by all means bring it with you. It makes sense to have
  electronics that are comfortable to use and whose
  operation is second nature. You can take it to shore with
  you and communicate with the mothership, too. Just
  don't forget the charger.
- Channel 16 is the universal channel for emergency
  broadcasts and establishing contact with other vessels or
  shore-based facilities. It is not a channel for conducting
  conversations.

ONCE ON CHANNEL 16, YOU'LL HEAR VOICE TRAFFIC RANGING
from boats calling marinas, restaurants and other boats to commer-
cial traffic such as cruise ships or ferries. So Channel 16 is a
common, shared resource. Be as brief as possible in establishing
contact with the other party before switching to a different channel
for the (still brief) conversation. There is a protocol to VHF use that
dictates that the party being hailed gets to nominate a channel for
both parties to switch to.

Let's say you are on the vessel *Rosebud* and are calling the bar *Rotgut's Redoubt*. Your exchange would be something like this:

- "Rotgut, Rotgut, Rotgut, this is Rosebud, Rosebud, Rosebud. Over." The response would be something like:
- "Rosebud, this is Rotgut. ACKNOWLEDGE and Switch to Channel 68. Over."
- Your response would be, "Rotgut, this is Rosebud. Switching to Six-Eight. Over."
- And you would change the channel selector to Channel 68 and commence calling again.
- "Rotgut, this is Rosebud. Over."
- And you would expect to hear, "Rosebud, this is Rotgut. How can I help you? Over." And you would make reservations for lunch or make enquiries etc.
- When you have concluded your conversation, finish by saying "Rotgut, thank you. This is Rosebud switching back to Channel 16. Rosebud out."

The object is to speak clearly, not quickly. Use the term "Over" at the end of each segment of the conversation, until you've reached the end. Then say "Out," to signal that you are concluding the conversation. Note the triple use of the restaurant's name and the boat's name, initially at least. In general use, you would only say the name twice, but if you were on the high seas and hoping to attract attention you should indeed follow full protocol and use the triple-term call.

Occasions for hailing on VHF:

- When calling a marina and requesting a slip or to pick up fuel and water.
- Making a restaurant reservation. A word of caution: In some areas where there is known to be serious crime we would suggest not using your real boat name when calling in, since that could alert possible thieves to your movements. Just use a simple name for the reservation. A

friend always calls his boat *Mango II*, whatever its real name might be. When making an emergency call, or requesting assistance, however, always use the proper name!

- Calling another boat whose name you know, or hailing your dinghy captain who is operating a handheld VHF unit.
- Responding to a call from someone whose name you don't know or didn't hear clearly. Use the formula "Vessel calling Rosebud, please go ahead."

IF YOU ARE TRAVELING IN A CONVOY WITH FRIENDS, OR HAVE another boat you wish to stay in contact with, choose a non-assigned channel—09, 68, 69, 71, for example—as a place to conduct conversations. You can continuously monitor this channel along with Ch. 16 and any others you wish.

Some areas give the weather forecast in French or Spanish only. The forecast may refer to the Beaufort Scale, such as in the French West Indies where you might hear: *"Nor-est, Cinque, Une Metre,"* (*Wind from the North-east, Force 5* or *17-21 knots, High tide—1 meter* Or *3.2 feet*) for example. When communicating with authorities, you will be expected to use the International Phonetic Alphabet.

Since bareboats get named the strangest things, it may be crucial to know how to spell out your boat name using the phonetic alphabet whether you're booking a table at a restaurant or asking for immediate helicopter evacuation.

DISTRESS PROCEDURE:

There are levels of urgency associated with emergencies. Some situations require immediate response since a life may be under threat from heart attack, loss of blood, or other trauma. But others, while serious, may not require absolutely immediate response.

Take the example of a vessel under sail and hitting a whale or some floating debris—and knocking out the rudder. The vessel may not be able to steer, or may have very restricted capability. Help is required but the boat is afloat and all aboard are safe. A third example is where you wish to convey important information related to safety, such as the presence of a number of floating logs or a sudden squall or waterspout of unexpected severity. In the first instance, the Channel 16 call would be a Distress call, or *Mayday*. In the second, an Urgent call, or *Pan-Pan*. The third is a Safety call, or *Securité* (pronounced Securitay).

MAYDAY:

Don't use this unless there is a life-threatening emergency—it could be a heart attack or a sinking vessel. A yacht aground on soft sand in calm conditions probably wouldn't warrant a Mayday. When requesting a Mayday response, you are asking for aircraft, helicopters, rescue divers—it's an emergency after all.

The person receiving the call will want to know a lot of information. For this reason, when going offshore you should have the information available for access by your crew. It's best presented as a printed card and kept taped to the underside of the chart table top, or someplace close by the VHF station.

We hope you never have to make this call but if you do, follow this procedure:

First, make sure that your VHF is actually turned on and tuned to Channel 16 — also, select 25 Watts/HI Power as you want to broadcast far and wide.

Wait for a gap in conversation if other people are talking and at the first opportunity press the *transmit* button on the side of the handset. Everyone else making routine calls will stop talking after you say the following words. If people keep talking, don't wait for them to pause but begin with BREAK, BREAK, BREAK. Then say slowly and clearly:

MAYDAY, MAYDAY, MAYDAY, then:

- **WHO** you are (vessel's call sign and name).

- **WHERE** you are (Your position in Latitude /Longitude from the chart or GPS, or a bearing and distance from a widely known geographical point.)
- **WHAT** is wrong (nature of distress or difficulty).
- **KIND** of assistance desired.
- **NUMBER** of persons aboard and condition of any injured.
- Present **SEAWORTHINESS** of your vessel
- **DESCRIPTION** of your vessel—length, type, cabin, mast, power, color of hull, superstructure and trim (listing, foundering etc).
- Your listening **RADIO FREQUENCY** or channel. It's important to make a communications schedule.
- **SURVIVAL EQUIPMENT** available (i.e.. rafts, survival suits, EPIRB, etc.)

NOTE: It is important that you give the full range of information since conditions could change and you lose power to your radio. A mariner listening may have a chance to write down the information or it could be received by a Coast Guard unit that records all Channel 16 traffic.

Release the transmit button and wait for acknowledgement.

Keep listening on channel 16 for instructions. Appoint someone to monitor the VHF for response.

If no response is forthcoming, then repeat the distress call.

Of course, if you should hear a MAYDAY call, *write down* salient details that you could pass on to the appropriate parties. Respond to the MAYDAY call to a) confirm to the caller that someone has heard them, and b) to gather information that you might be able to pass on by calling the Coast Guard on Ch. 16. The original caller's signal might be able to reach you but not strong enough to be picked up 50 miles away by Coast Guard antennae.

CONTACTS

All links are accessible from the website at:

https://wp.me/P9jJzL-53

BVI Search and Rescue (VISAR). https://visar.org/

St. Maarten Search and Rescue. http://www.searescue.sx/

Antigua and Barbuda Search and Rescue.http://bit.ly/2gBYbYT

Anguilla Search and Rescue. (Tel) +596 596 709292

St Barths Search and Rescue. http://www.snsm-stbarth.com/

St. Vincent/Grenadines Search and Rescue. http://bit.ly/2jwKd9S

RADIO CHECK

The radio check is an important part of familiarization with your equipment. It is not a test you need to make every day. Do it once on the dock and once when underway in open waters. The first test is simply to ascertain that the unit is functional. On the dock you'll probably hear back from the dockmaster who might be a few boat lengths away.

When at an anchorage or underway in the middle of a passage, give the world a shout-out and see who can hear you. You'll want to know how clearly and at what distance you can be heard.

The usual procedure is this.

- Set your unit to Lo (power), adjust the Squelch setting and go to Channel 16 where you say,
- "Any station, any station. This is Mango, Mango, looking for a radio check. Over."
- Ideally you will get a response like this,
- "Vessel calling for a radio check, this is Tuna, Tuna. Receiving you loud and clear from Turtle Cay."
- "Loud and Clear" is also expressed as paired numbers from 1 to 5 as in, "3X5" (moderate volume/maximum clarity) though "4X5" or "5X5" are the general responses. "Turtle Cay" is wherever the responding vessel is located. Now you have a good idea of the state

of the call and the distance it can be heard. You may get several responses. All the better.

NOTE: we say Ch.16 for the radio check. In areas other than the Caribbean we might suggest 68 or 72 but in the islands there isn't a lot of traffic on those channels so you might not get any responses. Ch.16 is a good option in this instance.

Chapter 12

WINGING IT

MAINSAIL MANAGEMENT

At the beginning of the charter one of the first decisions is whether to motor straight to your first anchorage or to proceed under sail . In some locations you'll even be asked to set the mainsail before you've left the safety of the marina. In others, you'll motor for a half-hour or more until you have enough sea room to raise the sails and trim them properly—considering you'll have to allow for a lot of extra room and time to sort out the new boat. In either case, you'll need to have the crew briefed and ready. It may be messy the first time, but you will all learn from it. And as with all things nautical, the more you do them the better you get.

Some items you'll need to monitor are:

- Is the Stack Pack unzipped and opened?
- Are the lazy jack lines loose enough to allow the sail to slide freely?
- Are the reefing lines free to run?
- Is the mainsheet slacked off enough so the boom can rise as required?

- Are the battens clear of the lazy jacks and the topping lift?
- Does the tail end of the halyard have somewhere to lie? —on the cockpit sole or on deck near the winches.

Discuss with your crew in a relaxed way any issues found raising and setting sail—or when performing any other boat-handling task. This way you'll come up with different ways of handling situations and the crew (*aka* friends and family) will better understand what is required to get the task done.

HANDLING THE MAIN: Generally, you'll have two choices when it comes to raising a classic main that slides up and down a track at the back of your mast:

- Raise the sail before you leave your mooring or weigh anchor, or
- Raise it whilst underway.

On the Mooring: Doing this in the shelter of a bay will allow you to get the biggest sail (and biggest job) out of the way in the relative peace and calm of a protected anchorage in flat seas.

This method also has the advantage of not needing anyone at the helm to keep the boat pointed into the wind, as in most mooring fields/anchorages your boat will lie to the wind already. So if you're short-handed, it frees the person who would normally steer the boat to do something more useful—like jump the main halyard at the mast, grind the winch, or spot the main to make sure that no part of the sail or any batten gets caught up in the lazy jacks (the vertical lines keeping the sail from spilling over the deck).

Another advantage is that there is no rush. You're not moving, so there is no danger of your running out of room to hold the boat head-to-wind. If it takes you 20 minutes, who's counting? You may need to pause to clear an obstruction or something similar—or to catch your breath if you haven't done any any cranking for a while!

THIS IS OFTEN THE PREFERRED WAY TO HOIST THE MAINSAIL. THE only requirement is that there be enough consistent breeze to keep the boat's head pointed into the wind—though if the wind is swirling about you can pause until it goes dead ahead again.

It helps to slacken both lazy jack lines at the mast—the sail may spill over a little at first, but it'll go up without fouling them. Once the main is up, re-tension them. While you can sail with loose lazy jacks, you'd better remember to tighten them before dropping your main, otherwise the sail will end up spilling over on either side of the boom. The heavy full-length battens on larger monohull mainsails make it difficult to wrestle the sail into position once it has been dropped.

On your first day, raising the main for the first time can be a challenge—the reefing lines are sometimes in all sorts of tangles and you might not be sure which lines are which. Open all the reef line clutches fully to let the lines run free. Take out the slack only after you're happy that your main is fully hoist. Before hauling on the halyard, check that the zipper (or other closure system) on your Stack Pack-style mainsail storage system is undone. Unzipping it when bouncing around in swell and wake can be a greater challenge than you need at that moment.

If you are on a boat with the increasingly common German-style twin mainsheet arrangement, with two separate sheets replacing the traveler-and-mainsheet setup common on most boats, you'll have to ease them both when raising the main to allow the boom to move up and sideways as needed.

The Topping Lift: Usually marked at its clutch with a *Do Not Touch* label, the topping lift seldom needs to be adjusted on a monohull bareboat. And your boat briefer will remind you to not touch it lest you crush the Bimini frame and possibly injure someone. That said, with the proliferation of large-roached mainsails on modern monohulls, the topping lift deserves the bareboater's attention, since it is now much more likely for the leech of the main to get caught by the topping lift, particularly when tacking or jibing.

Look up at the top of the mast before you raise your mainsail to see which side of the topping lift (port or starboard) the main halyard is led. The mainsail needs to be raised on the same side of the topping lift as the main halyard sheave, at the top of the mast—you don't want the topping lift crossing over the leech of the mainsail halfway down its length.

Raising under way: If you're raising the main whilst under power, turn the boat head-to-wind and ease the mainsheet and boom vang (if you have one). You want the boom to be free to align itself with the wind. If the sea state is making the boat roll, then partly tension the mainsheet to steady the boom.

Have someone with experience steer the boat so as keep the loosened main boom on the ship's centerline (if the boom goes to the right of center, steer left to correct it and vice-versa.) If you're short-handed, you could use the autopilot *Wind Hold* mode to keep the boat head-to-wind. Or just point the boat into the wind and hit *Auto*, making adjustments to the autopilot control as necessary. If you're quick, you should be able to hoist without much trouble.

Confident crew sweats the halyard to raise a catamaran's mainsail.

Many larger boats have power-driven winches for the main halyard. Be very careful with these since, if the sail is caught on a lazy jack or other obstruction, continued powering of the winch can tear the sail or rip out the lazy jack from its fitting. Have a spotter checking for signs of the sail's being caught up—especially the battens at the leech.

Station crew at the mast to help haul on the halyard. The correct technique here is to pull vertically down while it's easy and then *sweat it* by pulling laterally when it gets too hard to pull down.

Co-ordinate the grinding of the winch with the sweating of the halyard and things can go very smoothly. One possible difficulty with raising the main is that sometimes there is so much friction in the system—multiple sheaves (pulleys), slight kinks in the halyard, dirt in the mast track—that it requires serious effort to move the sail.

If the sail has a lot of roach (shaped fabric extending further aft than the end of the boom) make sure that the sail goes up on the leeward side of the topping lift. If the topping lift does cross over the leech of the sail, ease it enough for the leech to cross back over during a tack. Remember to re-tension it when finally dropping the sail at the end of the passage.

If your passage plan puts you on a course upwind—on a close haul or close reach—give the winch an extra crank or two to create a tight sail surface. When going downwind, ease the halyard a few inches and adjust as required for a little more shape.

Once the sail is up, the preferred method of dealing with the heap of main halyard in the cockpit is to lay it in a figure-8 rather than coil it.

Sometimes, if the halyard is extra long, it is better to make the figure-8 on the monohull's cabin sole, so all the excess halyard is down below—the same with reefing lines. On larger boats no person's hand is big enough to hold the resulting coil, so you may have to flake it on deck.

Some boats will have designated storage, such as a net or a canvas-like pocket, for the tails of the halyard and reefing lines, but they are optimized for storage with the sails down. So the lines can get jumbled together until it's time to drop the main when the tail of the halyard can be laid out on the deck so as to run freely through the winch jammer.

If space is tight and you have to choose between tidying the mainsheet or the halyard, favor the mainsheet and ensure it is free of kinks and ready to run in preference to the halyard, since you may need to release the sheet rapidly if the boat gets overpowered in a gust.

Chapter 13

PUFF PIECE

READ THE WIND

Sailing is fundamentally a matter of managing the relationship between the boat and the wind. Sometimes you'll see a boat cruising happily along when suddenly it sits bolt upright, sails flapping, because the wind has shifted forward unexpectedly and the crew haven't seen it coming or responded quickly enough. Likewise, a boat will suddenly heel over wildly and round up into the wind as a gust has overwhelmed the sailplan and caught the crew by surprise. These events are caused by rapid changes in the relationship between boat and wind.

The crucial element is the wind—you need to be able to feel it and, even better read it—since sometimes if you can feel the change, it's already too late. Better to see it coming and act preemptively. And yes, you can read the wind. All around you the sea surface is covered with signs revealing the wind direction and speed. Birds will always sit on the water facing into the wind, for example.

The clouds above, trees ashore, seaweed strung out in long lines—all tell the story of the wind and its direction.

The texture of the sea surface will give you an indication of the wind speed. And the trusty Beaufort Scale has precise descriptions of sea states and their related wind speeds. For example, whitecaps will begin to show at around 10 knots of wind.

Most people, of course can tell roughly which way the wind blows. *From my left, right, in front, behind*—good enough for a swing on a golf course, perhaps, but not for sailing a boat. A couple of turns of the head will be enough to orient you. Just compare the wind pressure for left and right ears—you can hear the *whooshing* sound as it slips past. When you have equalized that sound, you'll be head to wind! When sailing, take time to drop the canvas dodger—unless it's raining, of course—that way you'll have a much better sense of the wind.

Blind sailor Urban Miyares, says: "I get a short haircut before each (major) race and…I make sure to have a close shave. To include shaving the back of my neck, even though it may not need it… and it is not uncommon for me to have a tube of Ben Gay in my sailing ditty to put a dab on the back of my neck or cheeks before and during a race … In addition, on long-distance races, dry shaving is not an uncommon ritual I have before I go on deck." Unless, like Miyares, you have impaired vision, you needn't go to those lengths for a languid charter around the islands, but the principle still holds. Sometimes a simple splash of water on the cheeks or back of the neck can tell you where the wind is.

Reading the wind allows you to not only see what the wind is doing at that moment but, by looking further afield, you can see what the wind will be doing in just a few moments. By reading the puffs on the surface of the water you can see whether you'll be *headed* (forced to fall off the wind) or *lifted* (able to point higher). Good race crews hone this skill since it can indicate when it's the right time to tack—if you're consistently being headed, and therefore sailing further away from your destination, it's probably time to tack.

When sailing in the Caribbean, where many islands have steep hills overlooking the ocean, try at least once to climb the hills a bit and look down on the yachts sailing the channels. Observe the wind direction as indicated by the puffs on the sea surface and see how the boats react as the wind changes direction and speed. You'll easily be able to spot the great sailors from the good ones by the relative boat speeds on similar-sized boats. Not only will you benefit from the hike but you'll get a good sense of just how far away from the islands you'll need to sail to enjoy a consistent breeze.

The Air Apparent: Your boat's wind instruments can read both True and Apparent wind direction but are usually set to a default *Apparent Wind* mode which means that they are taking into account the boat's speed through the water (or, more correctly, speed through the air) to give you the apparent wind speed and direction. Without getting into the vector mathematics of it, what this means is that when you are sailing at 45 degrees to the true wind, your wind instrument will tell you that you are sailing at about 35 degrees.

Don't be fooled into thinking that you're a better sailor than you are, because no bareboat can sail that close to the wind. When going upwind, the apparent wind will feel (and read on your instruments) as being stronger than the true wind and when going downwind the apparent wind speed readout will indicate less wind than there truly is. It's all relative.

Chapter 14

CRANKED UP

THE FAST AND BALANCED BOAT

The wind can be fickle and mustn't be wasted—yet many cruising sailors seem to feel that they needn't bother about efficient sailing. "Why go fast?" they seem to be thinking, "we're cruising!"

But the wind can falter and die off, leaving you with miles to go —miles that you might have already covered had you been sailing fast and efficiently. It's not just a matter of sailing the right way, but of sailing the smart way. The skills involved can be life saving when you're making a long crossing or dodging an oncoming storm.

AND WHO CARES ABOUT BALANCE? "WE'RE NOT WALKING A tightrope, we're bareboating!"

But a well-balanced boat is one that sails smoothly. Where the helmsman isn't fighting the wheel to keep the boat on track.

That smoothness is the result of the balance between the mainsail and the foresail.

It's the shape and the size of each of those sails *individually* that provide the power for the boat—but the same shape and size *collectively* provide the balance. More power in the jib, let's say, and less in the main—or vice versa—will provide the correct balance for the sea state and the wind speed.

As your sails bend the wind around their area and shape— aspects you control by either reefing (area) or trimming (shape)— they provide your boat with power. You can change the shape and size of your sails to give you as much or as little as you need, depending on what the wind is doing and how fast you want to travel.

OF COURSE YOU'RE CRUISING, NOT RACING. BUT THERE IS STILL always the need for speed. You want to get to the anchorage or mooring field to secure the best, safest spot; you want to get to your destination early so that you can enjoy it longer; you want to sail faster than the boat sailing parallel to you, just for the fun of it.

Since you're on a bareboat, you'll be on a sloop with two sails. The shape and size of those two sails relative to each other will affect how comfortable the boat will be to drive.

All sailboats have a pivot point close to the middle of their hull around which they turn one way or another. A boat is balanced when its tendency to pivot toward the wind is exactly counterbalanced by its tendency to pivot away from the wind. Simply put, the sail mostly behind the pivot point (the mainsail) makes the boat turn toward the wind while the sail mostly in front of the pivot point (the jib or genoa) makes the boat turn away from the wind.

A tendency to turn toward the wind is called *weather helm*. The tendency to turn away from the wind is called *lee helm*.

WHEN WE'RE SAILING ACROSS OR AWAY FROM THE WIND, THE GOAL would be to balance the sails so that there is neither weather nor lee helm. But when we're sailing against the wind's general direction (sailing to windward — especially sailing close-hauled) this is not what we want to achieve. This is because sailboats go faster upwind with a small amount of weather helm. How small? About 4-6 degrees of helm. You can measure this using your boat's rudder angle indicator (it's part of your autopilot display even without the pilot being engaged).

It's when sailing close-hauled that you most often feel excessive (10 degrees, or more) weather helm. This, along with heeling, is one of your earliest indications that your boat is over-powered, meaning that the sails are generating more power than you can manage. A rudder angled 10 or more degrees to the centerline is no longer providing beneficial lift, but detrimental drag. It's also very hard on the helmsman's arms and will cause the boat to round up into the wind — especially during gusts.

SPEAKING OF HEELING, WHILE IT MAY FEEL THAT YOU ARE GOING fast when the monohull heels and the toe rail dips into the water, that feeling is deceptive, since much of the wind's energy is squandered in tipping the boat sideways rather than driving it forwards.

And modern bareboat monohulls are all designed to be sailed fairly upright. Of course you can't sail a monohull exactly upright in a stiff or even moderate breeze, but do try to keep it at a maximum limit of around 15 degrees from the vertical. Any more than that, it's time to ease the traveller (if you have one) or tuck in a reef.

Velocity Made Good: The technical skills needed to effectively sail a boat upwind and down—maximizing sail trim, steering accurately, following a course—are all well and good. But they don't mean much if you aren't able to get the boat moving towards your ultimate destination. The key to understanding how well you are doing in this regard is the datum known as VMG, or Velocity Made Good.

The *Velocity* part is easy to understand: it just means speed.

The *Made Good* part is also pretty easy to understand. It is just a way of expressing the speed at which you are moving towards your destination rather than merely the speed at which you're going through the water or, more correctly, over the ground below (SOG), since there may be current adding to or subtracting from the wind-generated pace of the boat.

The basic concept turns on the fact that sailing closest to the wind is not necessarily the fastest point of sail. So if going upwind, it may be advantageous to sail a lower-but-faster course on each tack. How much lower and how much faster varies with the conditions of the day, the type of vessel being sailed and other factors.

The instruments on your boat will be sufficient to give you the data—*Course Over Ground* (COG) and *Speed over Ground* (SOG)—you require to make decisions about the course you need to sail. And if you add a GPS waypoint at your destination and then change your chart plotter's screen to the *Rolling Road* view (scroll through to it by pressing the Page button) you'll get an actual real-time output of your VMG as well as SOG and COG.

Though, in simple terms, if you keep the boat in the groove upwind (footing-off a bit in choppy seas) and sail as low as you can go downwind without collapsing the jib, you will achieve optimal VMG—with no need for the magic box.

Chapter 15

GUST RELATIONS

DEALING WITH UNRULY GUSTS

The wind is not a constant force and doesn't blow steadily as if driven by a giant fan—not often, anyway. It fluctuates, sometimes quite dramatically. Many components contribute to these fluctuations—the topography of the land the wind is flowing over, the temperature of the land or the sea over which it passes. Sometimes the changes in the wind force are enough to knock the boat over, and sometimes they are barely noticeable. The good news is you often can continue sailing through a periodic gust—a short blast of wind—without resorting to reefing or adjusting the sail plan in any way.

One important thing to remember: as the speed of the wind doubles, the force increases by a factor of four.

Here are two simple techniques that you can use if you're sailing close-hauled or on a broad reach in gusty conditions. Neither requires you do anything to the sails. They work because during a gust, the apparent wind changes direction a little, as well as changing velocity.

Close-Hauled: The technique of *Feathering* means steering a little toward the wind when sailing close-hauled, taking the pressure out of the sails by making the *angle of attack* a little less efficient. The increased weather helm you feel on the wheel caused by the gust will want to make the boat steer that way automatically, so let it—but in a controlled way, so as not to allow the boat to get so close to the wind that you are in danger of tacking. And don't hold it there for long, either, as you may lose too much speed and stall—that is, lose your ability to steer. With any luck, you won't need to, because the gust will have passed by quickly.

Reaching: The broad reach is the opposite of the upwind situation. Here, you steer a little farther away from the wind. You're not *Bearing Away*, as you're not actually changing your angle to the wind and easing sheets. The leading player, the wind, has undergone a *velocity shift* and you must follow it. Be careful not to go so far as to jibe (or even collapse the headsail completely). As the gust subsides, your collapsing jib will indicate that you need to steer back further toward the wind to maintain the broad reach.

When on a close reach (around 60 degrees to the wind) or beam reach (at or around 90 degrees) your best gust management technique is to maintain the present course. Take the pressure off both sails by easing them out for as long as the gust lasts. If you're short handed, spill some pressure off the mainsail by easing down the traveler (if you have one) or mainsheet (if you don't). If you're fully crewed, ease both jib and main—but just as with feathering, the gust will likely have passed by the time you get around to the headsail. This is one of the reasons why you should always have the clutch of the mainsheet open—to allow for short and sudden dumping (briefly letting the sheet run free) from the mainsheet winch. After the gust passes, bring the traveler or mainsheet back in. If you find yourself having to constantly drop the traveler, then leave it down. And if you're still experiencing too much weather helm and heeling after that, it's time to reef.

Using these techniques, you'll find that the boat will become easier to control due to reduction in both weather helm and apparent wind. Plus, you'll be steering faster and/or closer to your destination for as long as the gust lasts.

Reefing: As we've discussed, sailing is essentially a relationship between your boat and the wind. In a charter situation, most boats are equipped with a set of general purpose sails, designed for winds within specific ranges—say up to 25 knots of true wind. The ability of the boat to sail safely in the higher ranges—above 25 knots—is conditional upon the sailor's abilities to control the size of the sails themselves. Operating with too much sail in too much wind can cause a multitude of problems. The control of the boat may be wrested from the hands of the sailor as the sail plan is overwhelmed. The boat will round up and it may broach—lay over on its side—pulled down by the force of the wind. Many Sunday Sailors don't get the opportunity to practice their reefing skills—if there's too much wind, they won't leave the dock or they'll drop sail and motor. But when sailing in semi-open water those options aren't always the most practical.

THE PRIMARY RULE OF SAILING IN A WINDY SITUATION IS TO *REEF Early and Reef Often*: that is, to reef before the situation requires it. Sometimes you'll be out on a breezy day and notice that over time the apparent-wind speed seems to be increasing. It was 20 knots, then 23 and it seems to be heading for 25. The steering wheel is jammed hard to leeward, trying to pull the bow down. You're wondering whether you should reef. The answer is always "Yes" in such a situation. First, what do you have to lose? You might spend a few minutes putting in the reef. Then you'll sail more smoothly and in less anxiety. Your crew will feel happier and you'll probably sail faster as the now more-upright mast and keel work together more efficiently. So then the wind drops down to 15 knots. Did you waste those few minutes? No, of course not—you can proceed happily along with reduced sail for a while.

See what happens. The wind may pick up or it may die altogether.

But it's always easier to shake out a reef you no longer need than to put in a reef you needed 5 minutes ago.

On the charter yacht you'll have roller reefing and furling for your headsail (jib or genoa) and mostly a classic up-and-down mainsail, attached to slugs that slide vertically along a track. In some cases you might have a furling mainsail that rolls up inside the mast.

Reefing the Main: Mainsails come in a variety of reefing configurations, each more complicated than the next. The more complicated varieties are considered to be more convenient—by the salespeople, possibly. Here are the varieties:

Classic Main. You're going to have one of three variations on the slab or jiffy reef system for your main:

- Single-line
- Two-line
- Traditional

All of these mainsail systems are simple, proven, and reliable and are used on both bareboats and the latest high-tech world-girdling racing yachts.

They all involve taking in a slab of sail by lowering the sail toward the boom. Do this by easing the main halyard and bringing down a new tack and a new clew to the boom and stretching out the foot of the newly reduced sail. (If you are uncertain as to the meaning of these terms, refer to the glossary at the end of the book). This is achieved by a reefing line running through a cringle (grommet) in the luff (front edge) and leech (back edge) of the sail, corresponding to the reef of choice. You will likely have two reef options: first and (deeper) second. Each reefing line should be a different color for easy identification.

Some boats may have a third reef—used mostly when offshore sailing, where you might encounter prolonged heavy winds. You'll see cringles for this but often no line, since it is unlikely to be needed when on charter. (If the winds were blowing that strongly, you'd have dropped all sail and be proceeding under motor—not an option when many miles out to sea.)

The difference between them is simply that the *single-line system* uses just one pre-rigged line to do the entire job while bringing down both new corners, while the *two-line system* uses separate tack and clew lines and the *traditional* uses just one reef line for the clew and requires you to go to the mast to pull down and secure the new tack by way of a snap shackle (a strong tape-like strap) or by placing the cringle over a hook.

WHY WOULDN'T EVERYONE GO WITH THE SINGLE LINE SYSTEM? One reason is that it requires lots of line—up, down, and along the boom—and, if set up properly, special blocks (pulleys) sewn into the sail to reduce the friction such a system entails. All of this adds cost and weight, which leads us to the two-line system. This also enables a reef to be taken in from the safety and security of the cockpit but uses much less line and doesn't necessarily require those expensive sewn-in blocks.

So why would anyone want to use the traditional system? Simplicity. Less line to deal with—even less friction and its associated menace, chafe. In fact the only downside is that it does require some intrepid soul to go forward to the base of the mast and manually secure the new tack to a pre-rigged fastener (often a snap-shackle or a Spectra strop attached to the mast).

Setting the reef: You can either stop the vessel by heaving-to and making your adjustments with some degree of comfort and leisure, or carry on and adjust the settings whilst underway at speed.

1) Heaving-to: This procedure has the benefit of turning the vessel away from the wind somewhat and reducing spray and other uncomfortable effects. Make sure that you heave-to on a tack (port or starboard) that will give you enough sea room. You'll still be technically underway and will carry with you the rights and responsibilities of the tack you choose to be on while hove-to so, generally, starboard tack is preferable to port. You'll be crabbing forwards and sideways during the procedure. When you have tacked the vessel with the jib backed, you'll need to ease the mainsail far enough so there is minimal wind pressure on the sail. Or you can:

2) Reef while sailing: Sail on a *Close Reach* point of sail (around 60 degrees True). This will not relieve the motion of the boat much, but will keep you off a lee shore if you happen to be dangerously close to one when you decide to reef.

- Release your boom vang to take pressure off the sailcloth.
- Whichever reef point (first or second) you've tucked in, you'll need to crank back up on the main halyard to establish tension on the luff of the sail.
- Then apply some vang tension—but not too much—as most reefs are designed to allow the end of the main boom to be carried higher, out of the way of the larger seas that accompany higher winds.
- If you've chosen the first reef, the second reef line (and the third if you have it) will now be very slack, so pull them in by hand and tidy them up to avoid their hooking around some fitting or obstruction during a tack.
- If the conditions allow, and once you're happy with the line settings, mark the reef line and halyard with a Sharpie so that you can easily replicate the setting the next time.

REEFING AN OVERSIZED GENOA: Self-tacking mono-hulls have a jib that occupies just the fore-triangle. But, if you're on a boat with a more traditional *overlapping* genoa, your first step at reducing sail should be to roll up some of that sail (10-15%) before you resort to reducing the mainsail. It's quicker and easier than adjusting the main. This 10-15% of the genoa—the part that over-laps the main (*i.e.* the mast) is a big contributor to your excessive weather helm. Take that out of play first. It may be all you need to do.

REEFING THE HEADSAIL: First, make sure you have ample sea room. Commence by easing both your headsail and mainsail and steer yourself on to a broad reach point of sail. You'll be sailing fast, so give yourself plenty of sea room. As soon as you fall off, you'll feel the apparent wind drop considerably. Be careful though—you don't want to do an accidental jibe! This won't happen as long as you're careful not to steer yourself past dead downwind (180 degrees). But you need to get pretty close (about 150-160 degrees) to that dead-downwind heading for the jib to collapse. This collapse is very obvious—the headsail appears to deflate and fold into the wind shadow of your mainsail.

Once the headsail has collapsed, don't fall off your course anymore (hand steer by keeping an eye on a landmark—or your compass if there is no landmark for reference). Or simply press *Auto* on your autopilot—though beware, as the autopilot can wander a lot if the unit's responsiveness isn't set just right. The point is that you don't want to jibe accidentally. Once the sail has lost its power, ease both sheets whilst maintaining control—though don't ease too much at once or the sail could wrap itself around the forestay. At the same time, pull by hand on the furling line until you've taken in the amount you want. Most foresails have short vertical stripes along the foot of the sail marking the reef points, so use those to guide you.

This is the same procedure as when fully furling the foresail, only now you are taking just a little power out of the sail. To complete the task, move your jib fairleads forward along their tracks commensurate with how much you reefed your jib.

SHAKING OUT THE REEF: Once you've decided the reefs are no longer required—the wind has dropped and is expected to stay that way, for example—you'll want to shake out the reef. This is much easier than putting the reef in.

Foresail:

- Take a couple of turns around a winch with the genoa *furling line*.

- Attach the genoa sheet to another winch. Arrange things —by tacking or jibing, if need be—so you're trimming the genoa sheet on the opposite side of the boat from the furling line. That way you can use both sheet winches at the same time. If this is not possible because of lack of sea room or other issue, just take the furling line back around one horn of a cleat, or around a helm-seat support, handhold, or anything that's conveniently situated, smooth, and strong.

The idea is twofold:

1. To be able to control the rate at which the furling line builds up around its drum at the bow without crew getting rope burns on their hands from the friction of a too-fast unfurling.
2. To avoid the furling line getting bunched up in a tangle as it enters the rotating drum.

- Keeping light pressure on the furling line, release its clutch and first begin to pull by hand and then crank in the genoa sheet.
- Trim the genoa as desired.
- Clutch-down and coil up the remaining furling line leaving it cow-hitched on the nearby lifeline.

MAINSAIL:

- First, go to a close-hauled to close-reach point of sail— around 50-60 degrees to the wind.
- Ease the boom vang and release all the reefing lines.
- Ease the traveler first (if you have one) and then your mainsheet(s) until the mainsail is luffing—that is, depowered.

- Start cranking up the halyard.
- Sail a little closer to the wind to reduce pressure on the sail.
- Crank the halyard tight and have the grinder, or other crew, keep checking that the sail is not getting snagged. And make sure to keep the reefing line slacked free. Once you're happy with the mainsail halyard tension, re-tension the boom vang.

BROACHING ON A REACH: THERE'S ANOTHER TYPE OF broach—one induced by a rapid increase in speed whilst surfing down a big wave on a downwind run. Often, in breezy conditions with a boisterous following sea, the wave will pick up the boat by the stern and send it hurtling down towards the trough in front.

Keeping your course, and not permitting the forces working their dark spells on the boat to dominate, requires *pre-emptive* or *anticipatory* steering. The wave is traveling a mite faster than the boat so its speed gets added to the overall apparent wind, causing heeling and creating weather helm as the mainsail/foresail/hull shape balance gets usurped.

The helmsman has to react quickly to turn the vessel a little away from the wind, reducing the apparent wind back to manageable levels. It's not unlike driving a car at a constant speed while going up and down hills:

As you approach the hill, you'll begin to accelerate just as the car's front wheels reach the upslope of the hill. If you don't, you know that you'll slow down below your target speed. As you reach the top of the hill, you'll take your foot off the gas otherwise you'll go above your target speed.

As the wave approaches, you begin to counter its tendency to force the boat to round up by steering away from the wind just as the wave reaches the stern. If you don't, the boat will accelerate and cause you to round up and be above your target course.

When you feel the wave passing under the boat, reduce your counter-steering pressure on the helm—which will be quite considerable—otherwise you'll steer below your target course and, once again, be in danger of jibing.

Chapter 16

WET WORK

HEAVY WEATHER

When we talk about heavy weather in the Caribbean we're talking about one of two things:

- Strong to Gale or even Storm force winds resulting from a major meteorological low (or high) pressure system. This is a macro-scale event that'll be well forecast.

Or,

- A squall. These are comparatively micro-scale weather events that will not be forecast any more than the routine Caribbean forecast of *isolated showers*.

WHEN YOU'RE CHARTERING IN THE CARIBBEAN, YOU'RE NOT likely to get caught in a hurricane—or even a named storm. These are tracked for days and well-forecast. Your charter company will have called you back to base or directed you to a safe haven before one reaches you.

Squalls are much less well-forecast and much more common. You are bound to at least see one in the distance if not get caught up by one. They can be isolated to a small area covering just a few square miles and lasting just five, ten or fifteen minutes, though it might feel like longer!

If you're observant, you can often tack or jibe away from an approaching isolated squall and miss it completely. Watch for vertical development and note whether the high tops (anvil-shaped) are directly above the base or inclined more to the left or right. If they're inclined right, the squall is going right (so sail to the left to avoid it) and vice versa. If it's getting taller and darker and lined-up straight then it's coming directly at you.

Isolated squall. It's possible to dodge this type.

THE OTHER TYPE OF COMMON SQUALL HERE IS THE *LINE SQUALL*. These are less easy to avoid because, well, there's a line of them.

But they too are often short-lived, despite their ominous look as they get closer and closer. Apart from the wall-to-wall line, these types of squalls are distinguished by causing all the local sea birds to fly away as, like you, they can't fly around the line. You can't fly with them so you've got three choices—plough on into it and get it over more quickly, heave-to so as to stay pretty much where you are, or sail away to reduce the apparent wind and have the gusts and waves on your quarter rather than crashing over your bows.

If the squall seems especially severe, it might be best to roll up the genoa and fire up the engine to keep the boat pointed as close to the wind as possible, feathering the main to basically hold your position until the squall passes.

When either one of these squalls gets close to you (about one mile away) you'll first notice a 10-20% increase in windspeed. This will happen before it starts to rain.

Then the rain will commence—lightly if you're on the periphery of the squall and it's giving you just a glancing blow. If you find yourself in the direct path of an isolated squall or in the inevitable way of an advancing line squall it'll soon begin to rain hard and visibility will go down to hundreds of feet or even just a boat length.

Make sure you have located your rain gear and a mask or swim goggles. The enhanced wind velocity and driving rain makes looking in to the face of the squall painful and difficult otherwise. Ask everyone not essential to the sailing of the catamaran to step down into the saloon—they'll stay dry and warm, and out of the working crew's way. Turn on your navigation lights and post a dedicated lookout.

STRATEGY VS TACTICS

No matter what theoretical or recommended strategy you read about and planned on taking (or that you practiced on your bareboat sailing course), the practical tactic you actually choose depends on the situation and on the skills of the crew.

If you have time, reef your mainsail. Double check the deck and get rid of any cushions or loose items that might blow away. Double check the painter of your dinghy if it's not in davits. Check kayaks and paddleboards so they don't blow off the boat.

NOTE: IF YOU ARE IN THE LINE OF AN ONCOMING SQUALL, NOTE your lat/long position from the chart plotter and write it down—you'll need to mark it on your paper chart. If you've brought your handheld GPS unit, fetch it and get it working—the squall may produce lightning and there is a chance your boat electronics could be affected. You'll need to track course and speed (from the compass and by estimate) and plot them on your chart—or use the information to create a dead reckoning position. You'll need to know where you are in relation to land.

Your charter yacht likely won't have radar or a radar reflector and while you may be a mile or two offshore, there could be ferries and other power craft in the vicinity. You might be traveling 2-3 knots even if you're hove-to—so put your nav lights on and keep a look out.

Chapter 17

PARK AND RIDE IT OUT

HEAVING-TO

Virtually all sailors who have received formal instruction end up knowing the same things, since virtually every sailing school teaches the same skills: tacking, jibing, points of sail, sail trim, man overboard recovery, and heaving-to. These are the basic building blocks of knowledge for any educated sailor. Of all these skills, the one that tends to get forgotten is the last. Heaving-to isn't a throwaway skill, though, it's an essential tool.

This maneuver is so useful in so many ways that it should become a reflex action for every sailor. It is used for managing a quick passing squall, as a component of the Man Overboard (MOB) sequence, as a way to gain a respite from rough conditions, as an occasion for crew to grab some sleep and a host of other things—in fact, for any time the vessel needs to be brought to a controlled stop while still under way. If the crew needs to get some rest, heave to and leave one person as lookout while the rest grab some shut-eye.

When hove-to, bear in mind that you are still sailing and you have the rights and responsibilities of the tack that you hove-to on—so all things being equal, starboard tack is preferred.

After the maneuver is completed, you'll be crabbing forward and sideways (leeward) at 1 to 2 knots. This sideways component creates a drift slick upwind that helps break up the waves approaching from that direction. Heeling will be much diminished and the boat's motion will immediately become more comfortable.

The downside of this crabbing is that your boat will still be moving to leeward, so make sure that you've got enough sea room in that direction. When heaving-to in order to get some rest or to await sunrise when making landfall, make sure you have at least 10 nautical miles of open water between you and the nearest land mass —or even the smallest shoal area.

There are two ways to heave-to. Your choice will depend on the direction in which you want your boat to drift. Decide which tack you need to be on, based on available sea room and the general direction you want to be going.

Here's how: Let's say you've been beating hard upwind on a port tack in 4-to-6ft. seas, no reef in your sails, the wind about 16 knots. You're the only one on board able to steer and you want to take a break. Or, you see a squall up ahead and you would be more comfortable waiting until it passes. Here's the easiest way to heave to:

- Sheet in the mainsail to its normal close-hauled position —at, or a little below, the centerline.
- Tack the boat, first ensuring the jib is trimmed in hard since you want to backwind the headsail. Make the initial tack very slowly: head into the wind but without passing through it, until the speed has really come down, before finishing the tack.
- Once through the tack, ease the main since, if there is a stiff breeze (as is often the case when heaving-to) the

wind flowing over the main may create enough weather helm to push the bow back through the tack.

- When you have completed tacking, you're now on a starboard tack. Your main has switched sides (as normal) and is now on port side, but your headsail hasn't swapped sides and is now set against the wind with its clew to windward instead of leeward as usual. This is what is meant by a backed headsail.

- To finish, turn your steering wheel all the way to windward and lock it by either fastening the center locking nut or by tying the wheel off with a length of small line. To make things clear, since you are now on a starboard tack, turn your wheel all the way to starboard. The wind is now pushing the backed jib to leeward—to port in this case. The rudder is trying to steer the vessel to starboard. These opposed forces allow the vessel to settle into a stable state, neither under sail nor simply adrift.

- Use the mainsail to control the angle the boat is making to the wind. By trimming in the main, the boat will point higher, easing the main will let the bow fall off. Find the comfortable point you'd like to be on—if you wish to create a slick to windward, you might need to ease the mainsheet most of the way out and go beam-to the seas —or even drop the main altogether. If you are rolling too much, trim the main to point your bow a little more into the swell.

Simple enough. If you started from close-hauled, you probably didn't have to touch the sails at all. But what if you can't tack because there's not enough sea room in that direction, or because crabbing that way will take you too far away from where you want to go? No worries, there is another way to heave-to that keeps you on the same tack. Assuming again that you're on port tack, here are the steps:

- Take all of the slack out of the lazy headsail sheet and (taking care to make sure that it's not snagged on a hatch or on anything at the mast) wrap four turns around its winch drum, then into the self-tailing jaws and insert the winch handle.
- While continuing to steer at the same angle to the wind, ease and then release the working headsail sheet that's to leeward, while grinding-in on the hitherto lazy windward one.
- Keep grinding the headsail to windward until the clew gets past the mast. How far aft you grind it will depend on the boat you're on and the size of your headsail. On most monohulls, you'll be bringing the clew just past the windward shrouds. On all boats, grind the sail in until it's stretched fairly flat.
- Once your headsail is successfully backed, proceed as above. Your boat speed will already have diminished so all you need do is turn the wheel slowly all the way to windward—to oppose the pressure of the headsail. If you have a steering lock that works, apply it now. If you don't have a lock or it doesn't grip properly, lash the wheel with whatever line you have. We use the tail end of the windward jib sheet wound between the wheel and the windward winch—you won't even need a knot—just wrap it around the top of the self-tailing winch.
- Once hove-to, the boat will have settled down; the pounding of the waves has greatly diminished and the boat is moving slowly and drifting in a smooth and comfortable manner, at about 45° off the wind.

NOT ALL BOATS REACT THE SAME WAY WHEN HOVE-TO. SO WE suggest you practice in smooth waters with moderate winds before doing it in earnest.

Other Uses for the Heave-To: Heaving-to can be useful for reefing (or dropping) the main. In fact, if conditions are rough or you don't have an autopilot, heaving-to whilst reefing comes in pretty handy.

- On a relatively calm day, when you want to have lunch without taking the time to douse sail and anchor or find a mooring—and conditions permit—heaving-to can be very pleasant, and lets the helmsman enjoy the meal at leisure.
- When boarding people from the dinghy—If some went out sailing whilst others went ashore in the little boat; or there was no mooring ball available at a National Park snorkeling area—it makes getting the crew back on board a snap.

Undoing the Heave-To: Just as there are two ways to get in to it, there are two ways to get out of being hove-to.

As before, the method you choose will depend on which tack/direction you want to resume heading.

Let's say you tacked into the heave-to and you now want to resume your earlier tack or course:

- Unlock/unlash your wheel.
- Turn it all the way to the other side. You will commence to fall off the wind and jibe the yacht. You may need to ease the main out a little to help the boat turn—but make sure to trim it in again as you pass the stern through the wind—and then re-adjust both sails after you find the opposite tack.
- The boat will turn almost through a complete 270° and you will find yourself back on the same port tack you were on before the beginning of the maneuver.

If you backed your headsail by grinding it to windward, here's how you get out of the heave-to:

- Unlock or unlash the wheel.
- Take the slack out of the leeward headsail sheet, making sure that it's not snagged anywhere at the mast or on deck, and load up four wraps and put it in to the self-tailing jaws.
- While continuing to steer at the same angle to the wind, first ease and then release the windward headsail sheet while grinding in on the leeward one.

Note: Perform these maneuvers as slowly and gently as possible —quickly throwing the boat around increases apparent wind and can overpower the sail plan in breezy conditions.

Chapter 18

ROLL PLAY

THE FURLING MAIN

No, that's not a nasty epithet, it's a term of endearment. With an aging demographic and a cultural preference for doing things themselves, today's buyers of cruising boats are opting for convenience and ease over complication and the need for large crews. Power winches and other systems that make short-handed sailing of larger yachts simpler—such as in-mast mainsail furling—while long a feature on private yachts are becoming more common on monohulls in the charter fleets. The pros and cons of these furling systems over traditional sliding cars on tracks are many and much-debated.

The reality is that you trade the efficiency and power of a large-roached, battened main for the easily handled, shallow cut, un-battened one.

The performance-oriented sailor won't like it as much, but a cruising couple or short-handed crew will find the in-mast furling a boon.

NOT ALL IN-MAST SYSTEMS ARE THE SAME. THERE ARE DIFFERENT manufacturers with different approaches—if you've used one before, or have one on your own boat, you'll need to pay close attention when you're being briefed for charter.

Problems arise when sailors don't use the system the way it was designed—and, hopefully, explained to them by the boat briefer.

Unlike headsail furling systems, where the sail rotates freely around the forestay and can get as fat as it likes, furling mainsails have to fit within the narrow confines of the boat's mast. Yes, that great big sail has to roll-up around a mandrel inside that skinny tube.

Now, if sails were as flat as window roller blinds, that might be an easy task, but sails have built-in shape (meaning, extra fabric) that gives them their power. Herein lies the problem that sailmakers try to solve by making these in-mast mainsails much flatter and by dispensing with lengthy battens—and the beneficial roach that they make possible.

Even with this compromise, the furling mainsail can still build up thickness as it rolls, and can jam—especially if allowed to flog when being furled. As with all furlers, keep an eye on the sail as it rolls in or out. It needs to run smoothly and not suffer from kinks or snags in the outhaul and inhaul lines.

Rather than raising and dropping sail with the boat head-to-wind—as you would on a normal mainsail—we recommend that you furl/unfurl a little off this (say 10-15 degrees) in order to get a more compact roll on the furl.

This method will also reduce chafe of the leeward side of the sail against the leeward edge of the slot that runs up the back of the mast.

Ease the mainsheet as you'd normally do—you don't want the sail to load up with power—though you do want to keep the boom fairly flat.

If you're furling-in, keep a small amount of tension on the outhaul to make for a tighter rollup around the mandrel. And be sure to follow the boat briefer's guidance on whether or not to ease the boom vang. Some furling systems are sensitive to the degree of boom angle (which is controlled by the topping lift and the boom vang). On bareboats, this is sometimes pre-set by the technicians at the base so, again, check with the briefers in case they want you to adjust anything before commencing to furl in or out.

THERE IS ANOTHER TYPE OF MAINSAIL FURLING—THE IN-BOOM furler. This more closely emulates the traditional type of mainsail—but rather than drop in folds on top of the boom, the sail rolls around the boom, which is turned most often by an electric motor. This allows for the inclusion of battens and a generous amount of shape to be built into the sail. Unfortunately the cost and complexity of this generally power-driven roller furler means you'll see it most often on a large sailing mega-yacht and not on a humble bareboat.

Chapter 19

DON'T GO THERE

MOB RECOVERY

The question of what to call the person in the water has colored much of the discussion of how best to retrieve them. Whether it's a man, woman, child or crew, the correct terminology is probably *Person*—but Man Over Board is still the most common expression for this circumstance in the English-speaking nautical world. And *MOB* is what the label on your chartplotter's emergency button will say. So we'll stick with those.

In reality, perhaps the most likely person to fall overboard is the most qualified sailor on the vessel—namely, the skipper. Because if anything does go awry on the foredeck, a fouled jib sheet, say, it'll be you who'll likely hand the helm to someone else or press *Auto* and go forward to free it. Things tend to go awry on the foredeck on days that are not mild and windless and calm, but days that are bouncy and blustery. You could easily find yourself in the drink with your yacht—and less experienced crew—sailing merrily on. If you are sailing at a conservative 6 knots, in one minute you'll be 200 yards/meters away. Ask yourself whether you think they could find you at that distance…let alone turn the ship around and pick you up in 15-20 knots of wind.

Sailing instructors are taught to impart the time-honored *Figure 8* and the more modern *Quickstop* techniques that are required in most of the different sailing certifications. They get fairly adept at demonstrating them after years of practice doing drills, week in and week out. When you've practiced a routine hundreds of times on different boats and in different sea conditions, it's pretty easy to execute a perfect save using either of these two techniques under sail alone. Access videos via web site at https://wp.me/P9jJzL-53

DURING THE TYPICAL WEEKLONG SAILING COURSE, A MOTIVATED and coached student can usually demonstrate a save—albeit under conditions somewhat artificial (they've been reading about it, studying the diagrams in the books, seeing it demonstrated by the instructor, seeing other students have a go, having crew mates who are expecting to serve in their designated roles, etc.) But this is not how things will be should you ever have to recover someone in real life.

In that circumstance, it will likely have been years since you last took your course and you probably haven't practiced it every year like the instructor suggested. Your crew may not have been on that course and don't know the drill. The spotter may get distracted by the tense commotion in the cockpit, or lose sight of a white shirt among the whitecaps. And did we mention the confusion you might be feeling as your boat hurtles away from the victim?

So what to do? First, relax. There *is* a pretty much foolproof way of getting someone back on board—one that is simple to learn and easy to execute.

If you're from the US or are well-versed in telecom companies, you'll be familiar with *AT&T*. Use it as a handy acronym to remember what to do should you ever find yourself called to action:

Assign a spotter. Have them stand or sit high up in a secure manner somewhere within your own field of vision and instruct them to point their extended arm at the MOB so that you know where they are in relation to the boat. This way you only have to look at the spotter and not frantically crane your neck to look for the MOB yourself.

The spotter must never take their eyes off the MOB or try to help in any other way because the instant they lose sight of the swimmer it can be very hard to reestablish visual contact. So don't give this person another job to do!

(At this stage, you could also press the MOB function on your chart plotter but know that is just the 'ground' position and the victim will be drifting in wind-generated current. But it will serve as a decent reference point if visual contact is lost).

Throw something floaty. The horseshoe or round lifebelt (PFD) that will be attached to the lifelines or guardrails close to the cockpit is ideal but it's sometimes fiddly to detach—so chuck some cockpit cushions as well. They should be easier to get to and large enough to see. Throw anything else that floats—cushions, life jackets, fenders —anything that will create a visual reference. You can always retrieve them later.

Tack. And we don't mean a regular tack where you throw off one jib sheet and pull in another as part of a smooth coordinated operation. We mean a *Crash Tack*.

Advise everyone in a LOUD and FIRM manner what you are about to do. Especially warn the spotter, since they must maintain visual contact with the MOB whilst the boat rapidly changes direction—the swimmer might end up on the opposite side of the boat, and the spotter's eyes have to be on them at all times.

Throw the helm over until you're sailing somewhere past close-hauled (say 60 degrees to the wind) but don't release the jib. To make sure this doesn't happen by dint of sheer habit, proactively tell your crew to not release or touch any jib sheets as you tack. This will cause the jib to *back*—that is, be on the windward side of where it normally lies, and countering the pull of the mainsail.

Once the jib has backed (it'll take just a second or two) and the boat has lost almost all of its forward momentum, swing the wheel over in the opposite direction to counter the turning force of the headsail. For example, if the jib is trying to push the boat to the left, apply full right rudder. Provided you've lost most of your speed (which happens within about five seconds on most bareboats) the boat will not tack back.

Lock, lash, or just press your thigh to the wheel to keep it in place.

You are now hove-to—your boat is moving slowly forwards and sideways (leeward) at 1-2 knots in most conditions.

Check for any lines dangling in the water—dinghy painter especially—and immediately **START YOUR ENGINE.** If you've left it in reverse to stop the prop from spinning, put the shifter back in to neutral first (if you forget to do this, don't worry as the engine will start anyway with no damage and a bit of reverse will only help proceedings).

Apply as many bursts of reverse thrust as necessary to bring the lee side of the boat toward the victim. If you're on a monohull, your boat will no doubt display some prop walk—pulling the stern to port (most likely)—so watch out for an accidental jibe. The key idea here is to use reverse gear to counter the forward component of your drift, leaving the sideways component to bring you alongside your recently overboard friend or family member.

On the monohull, aim to pick up somewhere between the leeward shrouds and the cockpit. Be careful that the boat isn't being blown down over the floating MOB. When within range, toss them a life ring or even a fender (attached to a line, of course). That way they'll have some support and crew can pull them closer to the boat. And be careful of the prop! A weakened floating person may allow their legs to drift beneath the boat exposing them to the propeller, so make sure the transmission stays in neutral.

Once the victim is alongside and the transmission in neutral, throw them a line or have them climb up the swim ladder if they're fit enough. Help them maneuver to the transom of the boat close to the ladder. They may need assistance to get out of the water, so appoint crew to stand by and help. If there's any swell, the boat will be pitching up and down and the swim ladder quickly becomes a hazard. There will need to be several crew available to grab an arm or try to get a length of dock line around the victim to help pull them up. Get them out of wet clothes and/or wrap a towel around them to prevent hypothermia. The combination of a stiff breeze and a wet body can reduce body temperature rapidly, even in the tropics.

If the swim ladder isn't an option, tie a large bowline in a dock line and have the victim slip the line over their head and under the armpits. Tie the bitter end to a spare halyard and gently winch the MOB out of the water. If possible, remove the lifelines so it's easier to get them on board.

When it is time to get out of your heave-to, first raise the swim ladder then free and center your wheel. Then, depending on the course you wish to follow, simply release the backed jib and bring it home on the correct (leeward) side of the boat. Or, if you don't want to go in that direction, leave the jib where it is and jibe your way out of heave-to and back to the tack you were on at the time the victim fell in the drink. (Have someone first ease and then tend the mainsail as per a normal jibe if you opt for this).

Practice makes perfect, so practice it at least once during your charter. It only takes a few minutes and will give you peace of mind. A wind-blown hat going over the side makes the best practice as it happens as unexpectedly as a real MOB.

Have everyone practise the drill. After all, the MOB could be you!

What about the dinghy?

Why not just get in the RIB dinghy? (Assuming that you're towing it, which you will be if you're chartering a monohull).

First, your dinghy may not have its engine attached. In St Martin and some other Caribbean bases, the charter companies insist that the dinghy engine be lifted and placed on the boat's dedicated pad on the pushpit, or stern rail.

Second, getting in to the dinghy in open water can be a challenging business—the dinghy may be bouncing around in chop, for example. The dinghy's engine may not start first time and in your rush to try, you may flood it. Or, someone may enthusiastically release the painter and send you drifting. And can you see the victim now that you're lower to water level?

Can you handle a RIB in waves? Get the victim back in a

dinghy? It's not as easy as it seems-- especially when the victim is fully clothed.

Then there's the dinghy propeller, which is just inches below the surface. Props and people are not a good combination.

So, **No** to the dinghy. **Yes** to practicing the MOB maneuver. It's a fundamental part of a sailor's repertoire. Hopefully you'll never have to utilize it—most sailors have spent years on the water and never had to experience a real MOB. But someday it'll happen— maybe to you. Best be ready.

Chapter 20

HOOKING DOWN

ANCHOR WITH CONFIDENCE

At some point, you're going to want to change rhythm and stop sailing! After first prepping the crew on the upcoming procedures and having dropped sail and tidied up the deck, you may be ready to stop for lunch or overnight in one of the secluded bays and coves that bejewel the Caribbean.

In which case you're going to want to anchor. Or it may be that you arrived too late to get a mooring ball or the only mooring ball left looks a bit dubious, then you're going to *have* to anchor.

It's not so hard—all you're really doing is dropping onto the seabed a heavy object that won't move, with a line tied to it that is attached to the boat. There are a few variables—where you drop the anchor, how much cable you put out in how much water, and so on. But really, how hard can it be? (*cue riotous laughter!*).

Well, actually it's pretty simple if you take your time—it may take up to half an hour or more to get the boat properly settled on the hook—and do it carefully. And let us say right up front—never be afraid to pull up the anchor and reset it if you're not entirely satisfied with your position.

If you're not happy with where you dropped the hook, or if you feel you're too close to another vessel or to the reef, pull it up and re-position the boat. It won't take all that long and the peace of mind will be well worth the extra effort. Sometimes it just means dropping the anchor 10 meters further ahead or a bit to the side.

Those small changes can have a big impact on how the boat lies to the wind and how much space you have around you. We have happily re-set our anchor several times before we were satisfied—mostly when we expected a big blow to head our way, but some-times just to avoid coming too close to a neighbor. It's no fun to be eating dinner with your neighbor sitting within earshot—especially when you're listening to some uplifting choral music and they're headbanging like crazy. Or vice versa!

Anchoring a Monohull: First, check the supplied cruising guide and supplementary charter company notes, which will tell you whether any anchoring restrictions apply. If you see no other boats anchored, ask yourself what might be the reason. You could be the first person to arrive at a less frequently visited bay—or you might be trying to anchor in an untenable or notoriously dangerous spot.

Your chart may have *anchor* (as well as *no anchoring*) symbols but your cruising guide will have much more detailed and useful infor-mation on the best spot to anchor in the bay of your choice. It'll tell you the water depth and—just as important—the nature of the seabed and what's ashore. If the bay you fancy isn't mentioned in the cruising guide, there may be a good reason why not—so don't assume that you're the first to discover a brilliant new spot.

Then again, just because it's not mentioned doesn't mean it's not a viable possibility.

There are many very good anchorages that are only suitable for one or two boats at a time—and sometimes the authors of the guidebooks may have chosen to keep some spots a secret.

But don't be too bold about dropping the hook in an unfamiliar and undocumented spot—it might be a very bad decision.

Next, assess the all-important wind direction. Although the general wind direction in the Caribbean is from the east (more NE in winter, more SE in summer) the wind direction where you're anchoring may be quite different—maybe even 180 degrees different.

THIS IS BECAUSE MOST ISLAND ANCHORAGES ARE ON THE sheltered, leeward side of a headland or other body of land and the eddies this land creates cause the local winds to vary from the general pattern. If you're the first or only boat in your bay of choice, you'll have to figure this out yourself, but often someone is there ahead of you. Aside from being an obstacle to avoid, this vessel is serving as your local direction indicator for how you'll need to align your boat before you drop your hook. If there are several boats, choose the one nearest where you plan to drop.

Catamarans and power yachts lie differently to the wind than deeper-keeled monohulls so, if there's a conflict, align with the boat that's more like the one you're on. And if the direction that the boats lie is unrelated to the local wind, that might indicate some current—which, while generally slight, may be significant at times of full moon.

If you have to anchor close behind another boat, don't be afraid to motor up very close to their stern. Drop the hook a few feet behind—say 10 feet—and you'll drop back safely and snug up. In the morning, if you need to weigh anchor before the boat in front is ready to move, they will probably motor ahead by a boat length or so to give you room to maneuver. If they've left the boat and gone to dive or hike on land, you can pull up close, with anchor cable reeled in and, after snubbing the chain, motor astern and drag the anchor free.

Overall, though, the most important factor when anchoring is to give yourself plenty of time. Arriving late to an anchorage and being obliged to find a spot before the sunlight disappears is often an anxiety-inducing situation.

Plan your afternoon arrival before you begin sailing each day. Set waypoints to indicate the passage of time—and give yourself an absolute deadline to make sure you get to the anchorage in good time.

Upon arrival at your chosen destination, if you don't feel comfortable about your options then move to another anchorage. Make it your practice never to arrive any later then 1500 hours (3:00pm). You need the sun to be still somewhat high in the sky— and remember the sun sets around 1750-1900 (5:50-7:00pm). You must be able to see the bottom in order to drop your anchor in the light-colored sand rather than the darker sea grass.

Scope it Out: The general rule of thumb for anchoring usually advises a 5-to-1 scope for chain and 7-to-1 for rope. In the Caribbean you'll have mostly chain anchor cable with possibly a few feet of nylon at the bitter end. So if you want a number, go with 4 times the depth (**measured from the bow-roller**) as a minimum. Bear in mind that some charter companies calibrate their depth-sounders to show depth under the keel rather than the actual depth from below water level. (Check with your Boat Briefer before departing). The bow roller may be a good 2 meters or more above the water line.

Point the boat head-to-wind or current as indicated by nearby boats, in order to drift the boat to a stop at the right spot. Use a short blast of reverse if you have to.

On a monohull without bow-thrusters you'll now be at the mercy of the wind and, if there's a breeze of any substance, the bow will blow off one way or another—so drop the hook straight away. Do this using the anchor windlass remote control or by using a winch handle to release the windlass clutch. The windlass will drop the hook slowly (about one foot per second/1 meter every 3 seconds) but using the clutch release will send it down like the lump of metal it is.

Since, in a stiff breeze on a monohull without bow thrusters, you won't be able to hover on station for 30 seconds in 30 feet of water, you're much better off using the clutch release to drop your hook—though you can keep your bow somewhat into the breeze by thrusting the throttle against a hard-turned rudder and using the resultant prop wash to straighten the boat. When dropping the anchor by easing the windlass clutch, be extra careful not to catch vulnerable fingers and other parts in the machinery.

WINDLASS CLUTCH QUICK DROP:

Allow the wind to push the boat's bows back and away while letting out more chain until you've let out enough—but snub the chain (that is, temporarily stop the chain by releasing the remote control switch or by cramping down on the free-wheeling windlass) if the bows fall off as far as 90 degrees so as to use the weight of the chain to bring the boat back head-to-wind before letting out any more.

Almost all bare boats have the standard 50 meters (about 166 feet) of chain so if you're anchoring in 25-30 feet (7-9 meters) of water you'll be using pretty much most of it, assuming the all-chain minimum of 4 times the depth. If your neighbor has the same amount of chain out then you'll all swing together, given that you'll be in the same winds and current.

Unlike mooring balls, where the swing radius is defined by your boat length plus your mooring bridle (and dinghy plus its painter), bear in mind that, when anchored, you'll be swinging around what's known as the *lift point*—the point at which your chain lifts off the seabed toward your bow. The stronger the wind/current, the closer the lift point will move toward your anchor and the greater your swing radius will be.

If you're anchored close to similar boats, with similar length of chain out, then you should all swing together and stay separated. Problems arise when you're near a boat with a profile different than your own. If you're on a monohull and your neighbor is a catamaran or a powerboat (which often in the Caribbean means a catamaran, too) you will have more boat in the water than out of it while their profile will be reversed and so they will swing more cagerly to the wind than you. This is a good reason to stay as separated as you can to start with, and also try to anchor near boats like yours.

Many bareboats have poorly marked anchor cables, making it tricky to judge how much chain you have out. Since you'll almost always have more chain out of the boat than in it, one simple way is to open up the anchor locker and estimate how much chain you have left. If you know that the boat has 160-odd feet (the standard 50 meters most bare boats have) and it looks like you've got 20' left then, ergo, you've got 140' out. Or, you could make your own marks in the chain with brightly colored cable ties (aka zip-ties) if you've had the foresight to bring them with you.

IF YOU HAVE DOUBTS ABOUT YOUR SCOPE AND WANT TO CHECK your estimate of how much chain you have deployed, you can try this trick:

Swim on the surface out to the set anchor. Then swim from the anchor back to the boat, following the twists and turns of the chain. As you swim, count your strokes or kicks (every second kick will do). When you reach the bow of your boat, start counting again as you swim the length of the vessel. Let's say you counted 12 stroke cycles to swim the length of the 50-foot boat—about 4 feet per stroke. Now let's say you counted 15 cycles from the anchor to the bow, which includes 15-feet of water depth. You can say you have about 60' of chain deployed, plus the 15' of vertical length and an extra 5' of freeboard. 80 feet of chain in 20 feet of depth gives you a 4:1 scope. Sleep soundly!

The Power Set: This technique both ensures that the anchor is set in good holding ground and helps set it a bit deeper. The key is to first let the natural forces of wind and current do their job for a minute or two while sighting two fixed objects (one near, one further away) at right angles to you. Then put the engine into reverse (with the wheel centered and locked or lashed) at the lowest possible revs (usually 900/1,000 rpm). Gradually increase the throttle until you are holding tight at around 1,500 rpm.

Once the Power Set has proved that your anchor is holding, rig a snubber line (chain hook attached to a separate rope) from the chain to the cleat nearest the bow roller to take the pressure off the windlass.

GPS anchor alarms are useless here as you're mostly so close to rocks and other boats that the sound of them rubbing against your hull will wake you up before your alarm goes off. Not to mention the likelihood of losing your GPS fix momentarily during the night —a constant occurrence—will mean a false alarm in the wee small hours.

Assemble and raise an anchor ball if you've got one on board. This black plastic folding signal shows—in daylight—that you're anchored, not underway. At sunset, turn on your anchor light (white all-round light at top of mast) but don't forget to turn it off in the morning. If, as is sometimes the case, the masthead light isn't working, try and make do with the steaming light and a cockpit light —that way you'll have a 360 degree white light showing, as required. It's not perfect but it's better than nothing. Don't turn on your red and green running lights—although many sailors do— unless you are actually underway. It sends a dangerously confusing signal to other vessels.

Anchoring Etiquette: The first boat in an anchorage gets to set the style for all other arrivals. If the first one decides to anchor close to shore and put a stern line onto the beach so as not to swing, then all others anchoring close by are expected to do likewise. If that first boat decides to swing freely to a single anchor, then the next boat can't decide to anchor bow and stern and thus impede boat #1. It's not a law of the sea, but it's definitely the rule of the anchorage. Unless, of course, boat #1 is a 20-foot weekender and boat #2 is a 60-foot motor yacht. Then the Law of Tonnage applies. Woe betide anyone who disregards it!

The best advice is to get to your anchorage early in the afternoon so you have ample time to pick your spot and to check your anchor by snorkeling over it to ensure it is set.

THE NEW ARRIVAL IS TOO CLOSE: THIS IS A DELICATE situation. On one hand, you don't want to be a total *Asterisk* by loudly demanding their immediate departure. On the other, it's not as if he's parked too close at the mall and you have to squirm your way out of the driver's seat—the danger is he might drag down on you in a 40-knot squall and break some stanchions, if not pull out your anchor with his.

If you are concerned about the way your new neighbor is anchoring, convey that information as quickly and clearly—and gently—as possible. Why let him drop an anchor, lay out chain and go through all the rituals that anchoring demands and then have you announce, "I say, aren't you a tad too close, Sir?" No—stand up and wave him away at first opportunity, though with sensitivity of course. Anchoring in a tight corner, we once had a French voyager shout passionately, "I have 100 hundred meters of chain. 100 METERS! I swing you all night!"

Not wishing to be swung all night by a florid Frenchman, we moved away. (Though if he really did have 100 meters out, had he swung to port he'd be 20 meters up the beach, and on the other swing he'd be stuck on the reef, but nevermind.)

Things needn't be so confrontational, however. Follow these steps if a boat motors up to you while you're relaxing in the shady cockpit on your own securely anchored boat. They signify escalating concern:

1. Look up from your coffee/tea/beverage
2. Give helmsperson a hard stare (as in *don't even think about it*).
3. Stand up with hard stare.
4. Walk to a point on your deck closest to offending boat (still with hard stare).
5. Fold arms (elevate hard stare to Evil Eye)

6. Place hands on your hips (arms akimbo).

Nothing needs to be said until this stage is reached. Most newbie bare boaters (even newbie boat owners) are unsure of their anchoring skills and will be looking nervously around at every boat close to them. Most will get the idea that they're too close by Step 3 and will decide to move further away. If they persist in anchoring too close (by your definition—not theirs) then resist getting into a shouting match. Instead, dinghy yourself over and politely point out that you're uncomfortable with their position as it's too close. All but the most belligerent sailor will reluctantly agree and move further off. You could even offer to help them based on your own newfound expertise—and so make a new friend!

If another boat does anchor close to you and the skipper shows no interest in honoring your entreaties, no matter how subtle or broad, sometimes the only option is to move away yourself. If this looks like being the case, plan your move carefully since the anchorage is no doubt filling up.

Don't leave it too late. If you are not able to move, deploy your fenders all around the vessel in case your neighbors end up dragging in the night. If you are truly concerned about weather and dragging, set an anchor watch overnight—station your crew on a rotating 3-hour watch from 2100 until sunrise.

Or, if the situation requires drastic action, stand at the rail and bellow, "I have 100 meters of chain. 100 METERS. I swing you all night." It's quite effective.

Chapter 21

PICK-UP ARTISTRY

MOORING TECHNIQUE

Moorings in the Caribbean are generally of two types: mooring balls and free floating lines with a float attached, such as a bleach bottle or a detergent jug.

Mooring balls are often associated with the better-organized anchorages. These are moorings in which lines or cable pass through a large floating ball.

These lines are

- the chain which drops vertically to the seabed and is attached to an eye drilled into the rock or screwed in the sand, and
- the pennant (or pendant) which floats free on the water, waiting to be picked up and attached to a cleat aboard ship.

THE PENNANT USUALLY HAS AN EYE IN ITS FREE END WITH A plastic or metal fitting within the eye. This fitting makes it difficult to simply slip the eye over a cleat, so please don't attempt to do so.

THE PROPER WAY TO ATTACH THE MOORING PENNANT IS BY passing a line, such as a dockline, through the eye and leading it back to the cleat it started from, so both ends of the line are attached to the same cleat. The same is done on the opposite side, so you have two looped lines. One running starboard-starboard and the other port-port. Simply leading a single line from port to starboard will allow the vessel to slide along its length creating chafe and causing wide swings in gusty weather.

When approaching the mooring ball, these lines should each be attached at one end and the bitter end laid over the lifelines, from outside the vessel. It is often easier to begin by laying the mooring line atop the lifeline and leaning over the top wire on the outside to secure the end of the line to the deck cleat.

The most difficult aspect of taking a mooring is the process of picking up the mooring pennant.

This is often done by the crew at the bow leaning over the lifeline with a boat hook in hand and snagging the free end of the pennant close to the eye and raising that end up to deck level, where the free end of the waiting mooring line is threaded through the eye.

ONCE PASSED THROUGH THE EYE, THAT LINE SHOULD BE PULLED in rapidly so the eye of the mooring pennant is fairly close against the cleat—say six inches distant—with just enough room to make the cleat hitch. Once made, the boat is now securely attached to the mooring line, albeit only on one side of the boat. Then the off-side mooring line is led around the front of the bow, threaded through the eye of the pennant and returned to the side whence it came, to be tied off in a hitch around the cleat. Then the mooring line first attached can be eased, so the two lines are of equal length, the vessel secure, and the prospect of the line sliding and chafing now avoided.

Bridle led outside Catamaran hull to mooring pennant

A SECOND METHOD OF PICKING UP THE MOORING—ONE ONLY possible when there is a mooring ball floating on the sea surface— involves the *operatic method* of throwing a loop of line over and around the floating ball. To perform this maneuver, a line needs to be attached as before on one or other side of the vessel, led outboard and over any obstructions so it is free to take tension without becoming entangled in the lifeline.

THE BOAT IS DRIVEN SO THE MOORING BALL IS CLOSE TO THE hull, about 6 feet off, and perhaps the same amount aft of the bow itself. With the boat drifting to a stop, a loop of line is thrown out and over the mooring ball, both ends still fast to the boat—or, in this case, one end tied in a cleat hitch around the deck cleat and the other end held firmly in the hand of the line handler.

As soon as this loop of line lands on the sea surface, the line handler pauses for a few seconds to allow it to sink a little, then pulls quickly on the end of the line—now led under the lifelines--so as to ensnare the ball and pull it very tightly against the hull, actually pulling it a little out of the water so there is no chance of the ball's escaping.

THE HANDLER THEN TAKES THE LINE AND TIES A SECOND CLEAT hitch on top of the first one, leaving the vessel attached by this one loop of line trapping the mooring ball snug against the hull.

THE BOAT IS NOW SECURE AND THE REST OF THE PROCEDURE CAN proceed as described above—the pennant picked from the sea surface with a boat hook. The offside line led through the pennant eye which is pulled snug against that offside cleat as before, perhaps 6 inches to a foot off. The line pinning the ball to the hull is now released and the ball floats free—the end of that line now led as before around the front of the bow, through the eye of the pennant and back to the originating cleat.

THIS METHOD CLEARLY HAS MORE MOVING PARTS BUT ITS advantage is that the ball is securely held against the hull of the boat, so the attachment of the mooring lines to the pennant can take as long as needed. In fact, the boat can sit happily with the original *operatically thrown* loop of line being the only one in play. It's good for a lunch stop, or to make adjustments to the boat, send the dinghy ashore for groceries and the like.

More usually, this method is employed when there is a strong breeze and the boat not easily held in place by the helmsman whilst the mooring lines are attached. With the loop of line safely around the mooring ball, the final deployment of lines can be completed at leisure. One person can perform all the necessary tasks —and in fact it is a good method for a single-handed sailor to adopt.

This operatic method (so called because of the action of the line handler in throwing their arms wide as they disperse the line) is as useful on a catamaran as on a monohull. On the cat, do most of the line work on the side of the boat which offers better line-of -sight to the helmsman.

One issue with mooring balls is that, in the absence of wind, the boat hull may tap against the ball—or vice versa—making an annoying sound for those sleeping in forward cabins. This nuisance can be stopped by hauling on the mooring pennant so the ball is pulled out of the water—it's the small chop and water movement that creates the tapping sound, so pulling the ball up removes it from these influences.

In some locations, the mooring line is attached to a floating plastic bottle, such as bleach container. There is no mooring ball as such. The way to pick up such a mooring is to lift it with a boat hook. These moorings tend to be less reliable than those with commercially monitored fittings such as we describe above. If you have a choice, go for the moorings with a ball attached.

Chapter 22

TIE ONE OFF

STERN LINES

In some anchorages—particularly very deep ones—it can make sense to anchor with the vessel's stern close to the shore. Often you'll find that the water depth just a boat length from shore might be 20 feet or more. It is often possible to get within a few feet of the shore and still be in a safe depth (and remember the tidal movement in the Caribbean may be only two feet, maximum.)

It is not uncommon to see several yachts lined up one next to the other, sterns tied off to a tree on the shore. And remember that it is the first boat to anchor that sets the rule for the anchorage—you won't make any friends if you decide to sit to a swinging anchor if you're in the middle of a group of boats anchored fore-and-aft, or with a stern line running ashore. Similarly, if the others are swinging on anchors, don't feel you can drop your hook in the middle of them and set a line ashore—sometime those boats are going to swing into you.

A small flotilla rafts up, stern lines led to shore. Image: Chrizaan Troch.

One way to check the suitability is to gently motor towards the shoreline, bow first. Set an observer on the bow to monitor the seabed and look for hazards. As you approach, take note of the depths as displayed on your instruments. Once satisfied where the limits of safe water might be, back out and find an appropriate spot to anchor so that the anchor is far enough out that it'll dig in—but not so far that you'll run out of cable before your stern gets close to the shore.

Once you are satisfied that the anchor is well-set, use two, three or four dock lines tied together to make up a long enough stern line. Bareboats don't come with long sets of line for this purpose. Don't use the kedge anchor warp, since you still might need it as an auxiliary.

You could use the dinghy to get the line ashore, or, if you have a reasonably good swimmer on board, just tie the stern line around their waist and have them swim it to the shore. Hold the boat close by using gentle reverse thrust against your anchor whilst paying out the shore line to your swimmer.

Sometimes it will help the swimmer if they attach a fender or other float to the line's midpoint. The seabed can shelve up steeply just a few meters from shore. If the line sinks to the bottom, the extra weight of line in the water can make the swimmer's task harder than it need be. The float will keep the line on the surface, lessening its drag.

ONCE YOUR SWIMMER IS ASHORE, HAVE THEM TIE THE LINE around a sturdy rock or tree trunk, making sure it is free of obstructions. When we say *rock* we mean a big, thick substantial rock, not something you might be able to lift an inch off the ground by yourself. And by *tree trunk* we mean something too thick to be bent by a single person—or even a couple of people.

When tying the line around the rock or tree, the knot to use is the Round Turn and Two Half-Hitches. *Why? Because you can untie it even under strain. Unlike, say, the bowline.*

Once the stern line(s) are pulled back and made fast to your stern cleats (or headsail sheet winches) tighten them by pulling yourself forward a bit, using your anchor windlass.

You may need a second stern line as sometimes you might want to keep from moving too close to a similarly secured vessel. In tight quarters, cross the stern lines in an X shape to further stabilize the vessel.

When releasing the shore lines prior to departure, first let out a little anchor chain from the bow. This will give you slack in the system sufficient to make loosening and then untying the shore lines a simple affair. Send someone ashore to release the lines from the tree or rock to which they've been attached. Use the final shore line to pull the crew member back to the boat.

If there are still boats similarly anchored close to you, use your engine in low reverse gear, stretching out the anchor cable, to keep from drifting in to them. In stiff cross winds, you'll need to quickly reel yourself forward to get out of the way.

Whilst this may seem a complicated business, it is really fairly simple. After having done it a couple of times, you'll be able to get the boat tied down quickly. You'll find you have created a great platform for swimming in the shallows, walking on the beach and other joys that are a little more complicated when swinging at anchor.

Chapter 23

SLIP TIPS

DOCK APPROACHES

Every year we see a number of world-girdling sailors pass through the islands. They are as salty and weather-beaten as you would wish, their vessels sometimes encrusted with oceanic growth, sometimes as pristine as a show-ring pony. They have covered many thousands of miles in all conditions; have beaten back the wrath of storms and endured days of windless ennui.

We have the utmost respect for these skillful sailors—they are out there, doing it. But whatever they have done in those many months, it's a good bet they haven't had to put their boat on to a busy dock very often. Now we don't mean to disparage the skills of the long-distance sailor but we would point out that

some of the best boat handling and docking you'll ever see is performed day-in and day-out by the dock staff at the big charter companies.

They probably couldn't navigate from there to the rum shop, but they'll back a 55-foot monohull down a busy channel and into a slip without blinking. Because they do it every day.

"It's all right for the professionals," you may say. But none of us were born naturals at docking and we all still occasionally make mistakes or misjudgments. We're often on different boats with different handling characteristics and the difference between perfection and an insurance claim is but a few millimeters.

Judging speed, distance, and the actions of other boat operators is a skill that can be developed with experience and time, but you probably don't have a lot of either. The only way to truly perfect your docking technique is the same as with anything else: practice makes perfect. Even a little practice will improve your skill immensely.

Check these points for information on the factors that come into play as you dock a large cruising boat into a slip or onto a dock. These factors apply to all boats.

Before beginning any maneuvers, be aware that there might be one or more casual observers standing on the dock—perhaps waiting for a friend to pick them up in a dinghy, perhaps just wandering the docks to look at the pretty boats. They will be instantly attracted to your approaching vessel—finally, some action!

Pay them no mind. Keep your attention confined to *your* boat and others that might get in its way, the wind, the dock, the targets on the dock, and other items. Any distractions from bystanders—who may know something about what you are doing, but often have no clue at all—will be to the detriment of your work. So go ahead and keep your attention to things that directly impact your performance. Though if a bystander shouts, "There's a puppy in the water," you might pay heed!

DOCKING

Here are the main things to think about when docking. Some you can control or at least be aware of and be able to factor in to your decision-making. Others are factors beyond your control that you have to learn to work with or live with.

Things you can control:

Prop Wash: The poor man's bow thruster. Most effective on a monohull with a traditional single-blade rudder. Use your throttle/shifter to blast a burst of water off the hard-turned rudder. This will push the stern of the vessel to port or starboard, pivoting the bow the opposite way, to point in the direction you want to go. The object is to push the stern to one side or the other to get the boat pointing in a new direction. If used in conjunction with Prop Walk, the boat can be turned in a very tight circle.

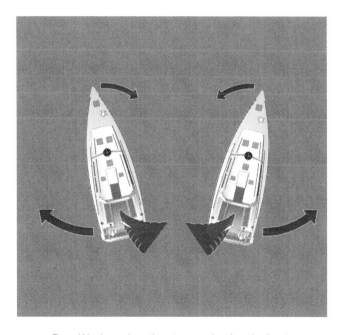

Prop Wash pushes the stern and spins the boat.

Prop Walk: If you're on a monohull with a traditional shaft drive, you can use prop walk to move the boat sideways. This can be to your advantage if you've figured out which way the boat's going to go—prop walk can give the stern of your boat a considerable kick to the left or right—in most cases, the boat will pull to port.

What it is and how to check if you have it are discussed in

Chapter 24. Boats fitted with a Sail Drive rather than the more traditional shaft drive are much less affected.

NOTE: the effect is short lived and only applies in the interval between the application of power to the propeller and the actual movement of the boat through the water. Once the boat has water flowing over its rudder, prop walk diminishes greatly and the boat can be steered in reverse using the wheel.

Pivot Point: On a monohull going forward, you'll pivot around a point that will be one-third of the way back from the bow—roughly where the mast is. When going backward the pivot point shifts to about one-third of the way from the stern—about where the companionway steps are.

Rate of Turn: On all boats, you can judge the rate of the boat's turn by seeing how quickly the boat's bow moves against the background. Use the rolled-up jib or a stanchion as a reference. Be mindful that there is an anchor hanging off the bow that could get tangled in the other boat's stanchions, lifelines, or other protuberances.

Arc of Turn: When turning while going forward, try to focus not only on the movement of the bow. Don't forget that the stern—especially on a monohull—is moving sideways, but in the opposite direction. The resultant arc is also affected by the fact that you are in a fluid and that the boat slides or crabs as it turns like a car skidding sideways through a turn. Be aware that, going forward, your stern is on the outside of your turning circle while the bow is on the inside. It's the opposite going stern first. In both cases, it's the pivot point of the boat that actually defines the circumference of your turning circle.

On a monohull, turning the wheel full over to its stops will result in a turning circle of about one-and-a-half boat lengths. If you're on a monohull with considerable prop walk, you can reduce this to about one boat length – but only in one direction – by employing the *back and fill* technique.

On a monohull with a bow thruster—providing that there's not too much wind—you could turn in either direction in just over a boat length using a combination of the thruster with forward prop wash and blips of reverse/prop walk.

Glide Zone: This is how far momentum will carry the boat forward or backward without any engine thrust. It will vary greatly depending on wind speed and direction—as well as your boat's own size, weight and speed when you engage neutral—as well as the cleanliness of the hull!

Check Your Glide: If you start your approach from a long way out, you could check the length of your glide zone by engaging neutral way ahead of time and noticing how far you glide while still retaining helm control—move the wheel a little to check if it responds. If the boat does respond by turning, you are still gliding, and still in control. If the helm doesn't answer then you'll need to engage gear and give a small burst of power for another couple of seconds to regain steering control.

Practical Application

Blades: On a monohull, you may have two separate rudders or the traditional single blade. As prop-wash effect requires a burst of water from the prop to physically hit the turned rudder, the single-blade rudder is the most effective since it is in direct line with the prop. If you've got twin rudders, the prop wash doesn't directly hit either rudder so the effect is diminished but not entirely lost. Your boat briefer will show you the setup.

THE DOCK LINE OF APPROACH:

- Reconnoiter the dock. Are there any dock staff? Call on your VHF to ask permission or receive guidance from the dockmaster, particularly if picking up fuel or water. Do an initial pass by to check out the space available. What's the dock height for your fenders? Are there cleats or bollards?

- Consider the wind (see below) and the available maneuvering space; circle back around to the starting point you've chosen to begin your approach.
- Looking at the dock, decide where you'd like the aft end of your boat to be when docked. Pick out two vertical objects, one in front of the other—a dock power console or fuel pump in front of a yacht's mast, for example. This is known as a *transit*.

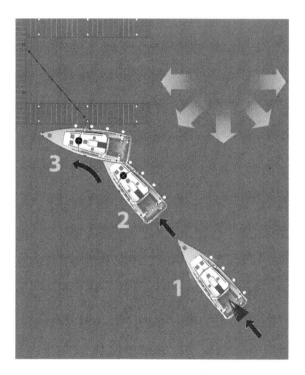

Create a transit as you approach the dock.

- As you proceed toward the dock, by keeping these objects in line you'll be following the right course. If they don't, steer or use your bow thruster to get back in line.
- Based on the dock height, set your fenders so that they protect your boat—neither too high nor dragging in the water. Most modern cruising yachts have portlights on the sides of the hulls so align the fenders to avoid them.

- Check your depths and the surrounding area on your chart plotter for hazards before making your approach.

Cockpit Conversation: Have a docking plan and discuss it thoroughly with all participants before beginning the maneuver. Turn off any music or extraneous sounds aboard your boat. Assign roles—spring line, bow line, stern line, fenders etc. Agree on hand signals and make sure everyone understands what is required of them—especially the spring-line person. Encourage them to ask questions if there's any doubt or ambiguity. Only then spread your crew around to their assigned positions. Execute your plan using hand signals rather than voice commands because they won't be able to hear you 30-40 feet (10-12 meters) away and over the noise of the engine, other boats, music from the bar (there's always music), and birds squawking.

Dinghy: Move it to the farthest side/end away from the dock. When approaching stern first, port-side-to, move your dinghy to your starboard bow cleat and on a short painter, and vice versa when coming in starboard-side-to. If you have issues with length rather than width, tie the dinghy to your outer midships cleat.

THINGS YOU CAN'T CONTROL:

Wind: We live in the air. We feel it around us and we see the effects it has on clouds, water, flags, and trees. We can't control it, but must be aware of it and learn to work with it. Observe wind direction and speed and what the combined effect of these will be on your boat as you approach the dock—and when you've come to a stop alongside.

Check your masthead wind indicator for wind direction at the boat and the courtesy flags on other boats that are already at the dock. The wind may be entirely different on your boat if you're 50 meters/yards out. Watch for sudden changes in intensity and direction—gusts, lulls—as you come in. Docks and buildings can create wind eddies and shadows, some are more exposed to the prevailing trade winds.

Docking with a moderate to fresh wind is like parking a car on a steep hill: if you're approaching downwind (down the hill) you'll need very little—If any—power, as the wind will push you. But, especially on a monohull, you may not have steerageway.   As mentioned above, check by moving the wheel from side to side to see if the helm responds. If it does, you have steerage.

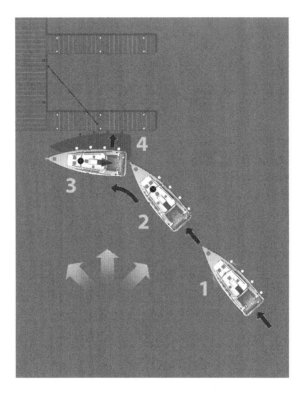

Docking with wind from behind.

If you're approaching upwind, (uphill) you'll need more—possibly constant—low power to keep moving against it.

WINDAGE: AT THE BOW, THE COMBINED EFFECT OF A SHALLOW forefoot (below) and high topsides plus a rolled-up jib (above) acts like a sail to blow you away from the wind. If you have a bow thruster, you can give it a short blast to leeward to nudge your bow back against the breeze. If you haven't, counter the wind's effect on your approach by either:

- Stemming it: that is, steering directly into the wind during your final approach. To achieve this, you'll first have to choose a starting point that will allow you to make your approach this way.
- If stemming is not possible, compensate for your bow blowing off by steering slightly upwind of your ideal line. The wind will tend to blow your bow down. Give the throttle a short burst against your hard-turned rudder and steer back up. Using this prop-wash effect you zigzag your way toward the dock, countering the force of the breeze.

CURRENT: CURRENT IS MINIMAL IN MOST CARIBBEAN DOCKING situations. The oceanic current is slight and most docks are situated in protected harbors. That said, if you do experience some current where you're docking,

bear in mind that water is 800 times denser than air, so just one knot of current is equivalent to about 10-15 knots of wind speed from the same direction.

Also, watch out for ferries and other boats at the dock that may be tied up but have their engines running and props turning—they can put out a stream of water more powerful than any current.

Other Boats: They were here before you, so you just have to work around or in between them. If you can't stem the wind directly, be careful of getting blown sideways on to the boats to leeward of your chosen line of approach. Close to the dock, look for activity on the deck of boats there—people getting lines ready, someone at the helm. A vessel might be about to leave and so make your approach easier—don't be afraid to swing by and ask them. And always check behind you. There may be someone following you in.

HELPFUL HANGABOUTS: YACHTIES ARE GENERALLY A FRIENDLY and helpful bunch and will happily put down their beverage to assist another sailor. They do the same for each other, too—it's not that you're an obvious newbie, it's that almost everyone could use a hand.

But there is a type of helpful hangabout who is not like these kind folk. You'll encounter him when you come in to a dock and the dockhands are busy or on a break and there are no working mariners around. He's the well-intended, clueless stranger who might be a first-time bareboater, a charter guest, or some tourist just walking along the dock to look at the boats—a doofus on a daytrip.

These people might be fine human beings who just want to help —but can they handle a line, tie a hitch, or know a cleat from a clarinet? If you have a plan and are confident that you can execute it, you can politely wave their proffered assistance away and say something like, "No thanks. Practicing!" We've seen well-intentioned dock walkers do the craziest things with dock lines. And bear in mind that you can say the same thing to the dock guys, the professional crew, or the Admiral of the Fleet. They'll understand. But you'd better pull it off!

Remember, too, that most dockhands have seen every imaginable docking variable. They are well prepared, so listen to what they say. If you can't hear the dock guy or are not sure of what he's saying, don't just ignore him. Use the phrase *"Say Again"* if you want him to repeat something. And give him (or her) plenty of time, since there are a myriad of calls on their attention: Guests wanting ice or fuel, departing boats, garbage pickups and the like. If you can be patient, the dock guys will be most appreciative. But be ready with your lines in place, fenders attached, your crew dispersed as necessary. That way the dockhands will be able to concentrate on the essentials.

Chapter 24

DOCKING SCENARIOS

SCENARIO 1: End of the T Dock (for water/fuel replenishing)

Bow-first approach: First, pass by close to the dock to figure out the design and layout—is it open from the dock's deck to the water level or is it enclosed? Wood or concrete? Look to see if you're dealing with cleats or bollards—and which will be your target to secure to. Confirm that you and your line handler are in agreement by specifying "the third cleat to the left of the corner", say, rather than "that cleat over there". Notice dock height for correct fender position; check whether there is a dockhand on duty, and assess what the wind speed and direction appear to be close to the dock.

Now swing back out to select a starting point for your final approach. Check your chosen wind indicators to decide where the wind is coming from and try to position yourself to make the easiest approach: this is half the puzzle.

For example, if a fresh breeze is blowing you away from the dock, start from a point that puts your boat directly head to wind. Let it brake your forward speed without pushing you off your desired line. If you're docking at the end of the **T** you can usually find room to make this approach even if you have to weave around a moored boat or two.

From the starting point, visualize where you want the *stern* of your boat to be when you're docked—and aim the *bow* of your boat at this spot.

Having chosen a target cleat or bollard to mark where you'd like your stern to end up, note a mast or flagpole behind it. Visualize a straight line between the point where you start your approach and those two aligned marks. This is your *Line of Approach.*

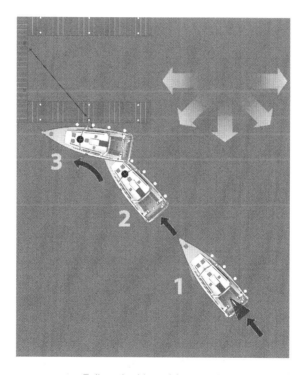

Follow the Line of Approach

Have a crew member standing ready at the shrouds, outside of the lifelines facing forward (if stepping off the boat), with a nicely coiled spring line in one hand, attached to your midships cleat and led clear (outside) of lifelines and stanchions. Instruct this spring-line handler either to step-off when close enough to the dock, *or* to throw a bight (loop) of the spring line over and around the target cleat (if the latter, make sure the line handler is inboard of the lifelines).

- If stepping off, take the dock line to your target cleat and, starting at the horn farthest from the boat's bow, make an **S** on a cleat (or two wraps around if you're dealing with a bollard) to snub the boat's advance, or surge-out some of the dock line. You should aim to have this line at least 3 meters/10 feet long—ideally from the midships cleat to a point on the dock close to the transom.
- If throwing a loop of line around the cleat or bollard and back to the midships cleat again, get an **S** on your midships cleat with the first turn around the horn farthest from the load—in this case the one closest to your boat's bow. Using this **S** as a friction brake, let the dock line surge-out with about 2-3 meters/7-10 feet and then finish it off by completing the cleat hitch with a figure eight and a half-hitch—or the **OXO** method if you prefer that.

Perhaps the most critical moment is when you turn your boat to bring it parallel to the dock, close enough for the line handler either to step ashore or throw a bight around a cleat. Turn too soon and you'll be too far away from the dock. Do it too late and...oops!

Remember that your boat's pivot point is about one-third of the way back from the bow. You want the widest part of the beam—forward, around midships—to be just a foot or so from the dock, so think about that pivot point as you get close-to.

There's no magic to this. Try making a dry run without attempting to attach your lines—just swing by the dock, concentrating on getting as close as possible without touching. Then repeat, with lines at the ready.

One variation between manufacturers and models is the placement of the controls aboard your boat. Some will have twin steering positions with the main position on starboard, well aft. Others have it to port. But you will be operating from the station where the throt-tle/transmission controls are. So factor that in to your calculation—if you are on the far side of the boat as you approach the dock, you might not be able to judge *distance off* as well as if you were on the near side.

Consider positioning an observer to give you information as to distance off, boat speed etc. Or position someone at the transmission/throttle lever whilst you steer from the wheel closest to the dock. You can then give instructions to the crew such as "Slow Forward", "Neutral," "Burst Astern" as required. You'll be gliding the final 10 or so seconds—move your body outboard, closer to the dock side of the cockpit to get a better view of what's going on. Your feet shouldn't be glued to the spot behind the wheel and, if operating the controls, you don't need to have your hand on the throttle all of the time.

ONCE THE MIDSHIPS AFT SPRING LINE IS SECURE, QUICKLY AND smoothly apply throttle in forward gear to create prop wash over your rudder blade, and thus tension the line.

Now, depending on where your midships cleat is located (they're not all exactly midships) and which way and how strongly the wind is blowing, turn the steering wheel to point your boat parallel to the dock. Even though you're not moving forward—because of the snubbed spring line—you will be able to steer the boat left and right as well as bring the boat in to the dock if the wind has pushed it out a few feet. If the bow is out to the left, steer right and vice-versa. If the boat fails to pivot onto the dock because of the breeze, add a little more power.

Twin-rudder monohulls don't perform this trick as well as traditional single-blade boats because of the lack of prop-wash-induced rudder flow. But they will still pivot off this tensioned midships *aft* spring line and the boat will be able to move on to the final step.

Once your boat is nestled softly against the fenders on your single still-tensioned midships-aft-spring line, keep the power on and the wheel turned to keep the boat parallel while your crew complete the attachment of the remaining three lines: bow, stern and midships *forward* spring line (remembering that spring lines are defined by the direction they take *from the vessel*.)

IF A MODERATE TO FRESH WIND IS BLOWING YOU ON TO THE dock, advance along the same line of approach, slipping in and out of gear to maintain minimal control speed. Glide more—in fact as much as you can since you're no longer fighting the wind—while keeping control. Your two transit marks will indicate which way you need to turn to make any correction.

Following your line: As you get close to the dock, turn the boat 2-3 degrees towards the wind to position the boat a little side-ways—in effect, alongside an imaginary dock that is parallel to, but 3 feet (one meter) upwind of, (off) the real dock. Once there, apply a short burst of reverse thrust to stop forward motion—allowing for prop-walk effect—and let the wind push you sideways to close that gap. Then get your docklines on, making sure the fenders are placed properly.

If there's little wind and current—or little room—come in at whatever angle you can or whatever makes most sense, since the elements (wind, current) won't affect you. Go as slow as possible for the same reason—no wind or current—and to make sure your crew can easily fend off any obstacles.

SLOW IS PRO: SOME SAILORS SEEM TO THINK THAT THE SECRET to getting a boat to maintain steerage is to have a rapid flow of water over the rudder. The result is a lot of high-revving cruising boats careering around anchorages.

That there has to be a flow of water around the rudder is true, of course. The real secret is to know how much is enough. Rather than engaging the throttle/gear shift and letting the propeller turn constantly, try slipping in and out of gear—say 2 seconds of throttle, then back to neutral. An easily driven monohull with a clean bottom can slide through the water for a couple of boat lengths with just a little push. By managing the power *on/off* ratio you can keep the boat sliding along at a constant speed but slowly enough that you can stop easily with a blip of reverse rather than a long blast (and its associated prop-walk effect). This is what is meant by Minimal Control Speed (MCS).

Use your bow-thruster if you have one. Again, just a brief burst to align your sharp end to the right direction.

STERN-FIRST APPROACH: WHEN COMING INTO A FINGER PIER OR slip for the night, the common preference is to come in stern-to, because it makes connecting shore-power cables much simpler. Driving astern scares many new sailors, but is actually easier than steering in forward.

With the rudder and propeller almost directly beneath the helmsman's feet, the stern is the leading point of the curve described by the turn. The boat's pivot point moves further aft, closer to the companionway steps. With the steering gear providing underwater resistance, wind effect is reduced so turns are tighter.

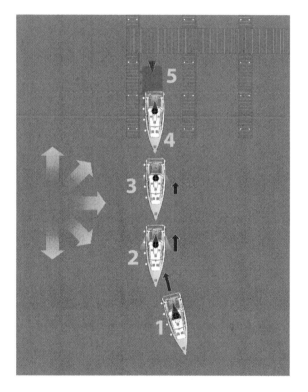

Use minimal forward thrust to stop the boat.

YOU'LL STILL WANT A MIDSHIPS SPRING LINE—THIS TIME A forward spring. But, unlike coming in bow-first, you won't be able to use forward gear prop wash against your rudder to keep you pinned parallel to the dock. Instead, use a blip of forward gear to stop your continued sternward movement and be prepared to get your dock-lines—especially your bow and stern lines—on quickly.

NOTE: MAKE SURE THAT ALL THE LINES ARE ON THE CORRECT (outboard) side of all of the ship's metalwork (pulpits, stern rail/pushpits, stanchions and lifelines.)

And go easy on the throttle. Every time you employ reverse gear you're going to get some prop walk effect that may not be helpful.

SOME HINTS TO AID YOU WHEN DOCKING STERN FIRST: GIVE yourself a long approach to your dock. Go way further out than you might think necessary (four boat lengths or more) so that you can glide in neutral the last two boat lengths without needing to engage reverse gear with its prop walk effect.

- Before you start going backwards, pre-angle your boat to allow for the stern's sideways kick before the boat has begun making sternway through the water.
- Remember that your pivot point is now at the companionway.
- Stand sideways, facing outboard (if your boat's cockpit allows), with each knee on either side of the wheel. This way you can easily glance in the direction you're going and at the rate of turn of your bow, which will be exaggerated because of the new pivot point.
- Once you're going astern at a good rate (about 2 knots) put the engine into neutral and glide in without using any more reverse/prop walk. If you do need more

sternward power, ease the boat in and out of gear gently and briefly—this way you'll avoid too much sideways stern kick.

- If you can't find space for a long run-up, driving in reverse will require the in-and-out method of shifter/throttle. This is especially apparent when there is a good deal of prop walk—you may need to maintain a steady application of power.
- If you're on a monohull with a Sail Drive unit there will be minimal prop walk, so driving astern with an intermittent application of power is much simpler than with a conventional drive train.
- When driving astern, keep a firm grip on the wheel, since the pressure of the water passing over the rudder can quickly take control and slam it to one side or the other, potentially weakening or breaking steering cables.

ONCE DOCKED: ONCE SECURED TO THE DOCK WITH INITIAL, lassoed dock lines, re-tie them to single lines—to reduce chafe and ensure that a temporarily eased bight doesn't slip off. Either leave a neatly wound coil on the dock or do it *ship style* meaning one line/one job—with the bitter end on the dock and the rest taken back to the ship.

Just before departing, double-up these lines back to the ship again so that they can be released from the deck and so avoid unnecessary leaps from the dock on to the boat. Try to retrieve those lines quickly if they drop in to the water for two reasons:

- Once they're wet they are much heavier to handle, and
- You don't want them around a spinning prop or bow thruster!

NOTE: WHEN PLUGGING IN POWER CORDS, TAKE A TURN AROUND a nearby cleat on both the boat side and dock side to make sure that the connector ends don't go in the water or pull out of the socket. The correct order is to attach the boat-side socket first, then the shore-side socket. Only then should you flick on the breaker at the dock. Make sure all AC-driven utilities, such as air conditioning and battery charger, are turned off at the breaker panel before you activate the shore-power supply at the dock-side electrical panel.

Chapter 25

WALK THE WALK

PROP WALK

Prop Walk is the term that describes the tendency of the stern of the vessel to pull to either port or starboard when reverse gear is engaged. This phenomenon can be quite pronounced, with the boat beginning to describe a circle as the transmission is engaged in reverse, or it might be slight—each boat is different.

It occurs only when the vessel is starting from rest or when it has slowed sufficiently that there is no longer a significant amount of water flowing over the rudder. The effect lasts until there is enough sternway to create water flow. Once there is such flow, the rudder exerts control and the vessel can be steered normally. For the majority of boats, the prop walk pulls the stern of the vessel to port. In a few instances, the pull is to starboard. It is essential for the operator to understand how prop walk works and how to best use its effects.

First, this phenomenon is unique to monohulls—of all varieties, power as well as sail. Powerboat owners with single-prop inboards will experience the effect as much as a sailor on a 50-footer. There are many theories regarding the reasons behind prop walk, not all of them convincing. The best way to think of it is that the propeller, in reverse, is a fairly blunt instrument, its blades—optimized for forward propulsion by way of curvature—are less efficient when revolving in the opposite direction. When the propeller is turning backwards, the relative inefficiency means that the turning effect creates a kind of paddlewheel, which pulls the stern of the vessel in the direction of rotation. Most single-engined sailboats have a right-hand propeller, which turns in a clockwise motion when going forward as viewed from behind the vessel. That same propeller will turn counter-clockwise when going astern, albeit inefficiently, thus pulling the stern to port.

You can check your boat's prop walk tendencies at the dock before you leave by engaging slow reverse while securely tied to the dock—first making sure that your spring lines have no slack in them —and looking over both sides of the boat forward of the cockpit to see on which side the prop wash appears. If you see the stream of water rushing forward on your starboard side, you have a right-handed prop and your stern is kicking to port—or would be, if you weren't attached to the dock. If the stream is directed to the port side, you have an unusual left-handed prop—and your transmission turns in a counter-clockwise direction of course—while your stern kicks to starboard.

You can use this attribute when docking your boat. If approaching the dock port-side to—nice and slowly—a short burst in reverse can pull the stern into the dock and make the line-handlers' jobs a little easier. With a left-handed prop, the opposite would be true and you would dock starboard-side to.

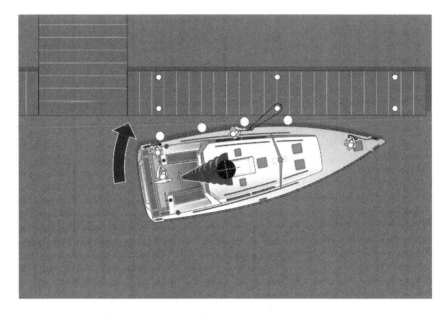

Use prop walk to pull the stern close to the dock

The main thing, though, is to be aware of all the dynamic influences on the boat. Unlike a car, which is attached by friction to a solid surface and can be reliably braked and steered to go where directed, your boat's underbody is floating in one fluid, with its topsides and rig affected by another moving fluid. With forethought and some practice, much of what happens on and to the boat becomes predictable and—more important—useable. So turn the mechanical effects of prop walk and prop wash to your advantage— and use bow thrusters when you have them. When it's favorable, let the wind blow you onto or off the dock. Let Nature do the work— it's easier that way.

Chapter 26

ONE GOOD TURN

BACK AND FILL

We previously described *Prop Walk* and its complications but here we'd like to discuss its advantages. These are highly specialized, in that the advantage of Prop Walk lies in allowing us to complete a tight turn in a maneuver known as a *Back and Fill*. Sometimes known as a *Standing Turn*, it can be compared (very loosely) to a 3-point turn in a car.

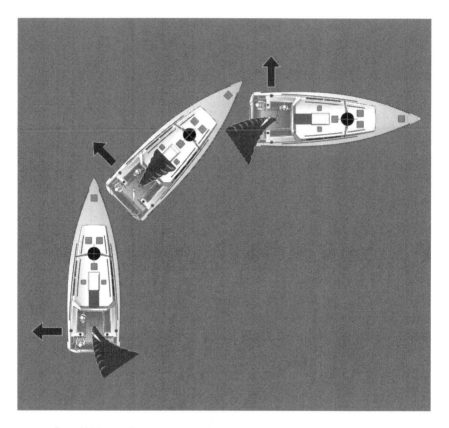

Prop Walk and Prop Wash combine to turn the boat in a short length

This technique will turn your monohull in about one boat length and is useful in getting you out of a tight spot or to set you up for a mooring pick-up or to drop the anchor in a specific spot.

First, know which way Prop Walk will pull your stern. Most likely it's to port, so you'll look at doing a *Back and Fill* while turning to starboard. From powering dead ahead, swing the wheel hard over to starboard until it reaches its limiting stops.

Shift the transmission to neutral as the boat swings to starboard, shedding some velocity. After pausing in neutral briefly, ease your transmission into reverse. Leave the rudder turned hard to starboard. The rudder has no effect on this part of the maneuver.

Now you'll use Prop Walk to your advantage as the paddle wheel effect pulls your stern to port, greatly reducing your turning circle. Before your boat begins to move backward, shift out of reverse and back into neutral. The reverse segment needs only to be a short burst, just a couple of seconds.

Now give your throttle/shifter control a quick burst in forward. The resulting pulse of water against your hard-turned rudder will further turn the bow to starboard, in the effect known as Prop Wash.

Shift back into reverse gear (after pausing in neutral) and give another quick burst in reverse, reviving the Prop Walk effect and moving the stern to port again. Around you go!

You'll find that you can make a tight turn in significantly less distance compared with using rudder alone.

WHEN SHOULD YOU USE THIS TECHNIQUE? OFTEN IT COMES IN handy when departing from a slip or a mooring and you have to make a quick turn to clear the opposite dock or another boat or mooring. But plan ahead, since your Back-and-Fill will only work in one direction.

But it comes in handy any time you wish to turn the boat quickly—after dropping sail, when dropping anchor, picking up an anchor, approaching a mooring ball, or lining up in order to reverse into a slip. The more you practice it, the more you'll identify opportunities for its use.

If you have to turn in a direction where Prop Walk won't assist you, use the *Prop Wash* technique to sharpen your turn. Use your throttle/shifter to blast a pulse of water off the hard-turned rudder, pushing the stern away from, and the bow towards, your desired direction. You can make multiple short thrusts on the throttle, sending pulses of accelerated water against the hard-turned rudder —in this case, to port rather than to starboard. If the pulses are short the boat won't make much forward progress, but will be pivoted into a tight turn.

On all monohulls that you'll charter, the propeller will be forward of the rudder. But where they differ depends on whether you have one single rudder, or twin rudders offset to either side of the hull, away from the flow of water from the propeller. Though not nearly as responsive as with a full single-blade rudder, a quick burst on the throttle can still get a decent response by pushing the boat forward and creating water flow over the twin blades. Spend some time and practice these techniques—they will come in very handy during your charter.

.

Chapter 27

COWBOY UP

THROWING A BIGHT

When approaching a dock, the best technique for attaching a dockline to a cleat or bollard varies depending on the type of boat. The main difference lies in whether it is safer and easier to stay aboard the vessel than to step off onto the dock. As cruising boats have increased in size—not overall length necessarily, but interior volume definitely—freeboard has increased as well. This is now as true for monohulls as for catamarans, which have almost always sported high topsides.

What used to be an easy step down from the deck to the dock is now often a heart-stopping leap, accompanied by the risk of a twisted ankle or knee, the dropping of the line or a staggering waltz around the (inevitable) group of bemused bystanders. So what's the alternative?

The best option is to stay aboard the vessel and throw (or drop) a loop of line—a bight—from the deck down to and around the dockside cleat or bollard, then to secure the free end back on deck, around the originating cleat. The method for throwing the line is often described as throwing a *Lasso*—though it differs from the cowboy version in that the loop that is thrown is an open loop and not a closed one.

Don't let go as you throw

THE ORDER OF EVENTS IS AS FOLLOWS:

- First, if your boat has docklines with a pre-spliced or pre-made loop in one end, slide it through-and-over the cleat (from the outside). If not, make a bowline and do the same.
- Having thus secured the end to the cleat on board your vessel—at bow or stern on a catamaran and also midships on a monohull—then coil it toward the bitter (unattached) end, making several loops of a full arms length apart and each made with a half-roll (away from you).
- Divide these assembled loops neatly in two so that half of them are in one hand, and half in the other.
- Make sure the line is free to run and not entangled in lifelines or other metalwork.

THERE ARE TWO WAYS OF CASTING OFF YOUR LOOPS. IF YOU'RE the line thrower, your choice will depend on how close the driver can bring the boat to the target cleat, and your height and arm strength.

The Backswing Method:

Let's say that the person driving the boat is being very cautious, or hasn't been able to bring you as close to your target as you'd like. Provided you're no further than about ten feet (3 meters) away you can still probably get your bight home by standing somewhat sideways (inboard or outboard depending if you're right or left-handed) and employing a backswing to both sets of loops. Do two or three swings to establish a rhythm. But make sure that no lifelines are in the way of your swing. On all bareboats, one of the side, and all of the aft, lifelines will have detachable clips, enabling you to have more room to swing your loops. On some catamarans, the forward lifelines are also detachable.

THE OPERATIC METHOD:

This is for shorter throws, where the driver has got you, the line-thrower, to within six feet (2 meters) of your target. Here, the loops in the other hand should be held loosely as well, with palms facing inward—toward your chest. Now bring both the hands, with the loops of line held securely, together at chest level, just touching the sternum. Then fling both hands out wide, releasing the loops of line when your arms are fully extended. Think of a tenor throwing out his arms at the end of a performance.

IMPORTANT: In both these methods, the loops of line are released at the end of the front swing as the arms reach their full extension so that all is released. But the line is STILL FIRMLY GRASPED AT THE BITTER END BY THE FINGERS OF THE RELEASING HAND. Just before you make your final approach, try to practice by making a few dummy throws inboard into your boat to keep the line dry—you'll be surprised how far you can cast! This way, you'll throw with greater confidence of your range.

NOTE: Never aim *at* your target cleat or bollard. Always aim *beyond* it and you should get it first time.

The thrower must now rapidly gather the line back aboard the vessel, and having made it as short as possible, quickly make it fast around the cleat it started from in the usual fashion, creating a tight loop around the dockside target—the shorter, the better. But they need to get it on as fast as they can, since the driver can't perform his next maneuver until they do.

On a monohull with the line lassoed from the midships cleat, the driver should engage low forward gear and use the now-taut line to pivot the boat parallel to the dock.

After the remaining bow and spring lines are leisurely *lassoed* in the same way, the boat, now secured, can be left with the lines exactly as is for a short time whilst refueling or shopping. For a longer stay they should be retied with the working end on the dock and the bitter end attached to the boat's cleats.

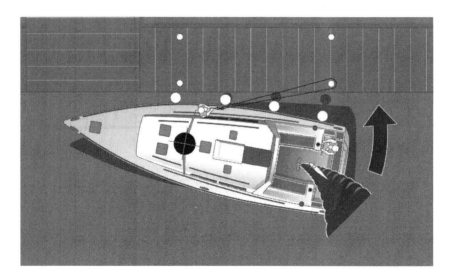

Pivot off a midships aft spring line.

If the thrown line doesn't initially loop properly around the dockside cleat, it can be pulled back aboard and re-thrown as described above. This can be repeated several times—even if it means maneuvering the boat away from the dock and returning to position it as close as desired. In this way, there is no one left waiting on the dock.

Chapter 28

BEACH BUGGY

THE DINGHY

The Dink, the skiff, the runabout, the station wagon, the shore boat, the taxi—has many names and many purposes. The cheery nicknames endorse just how important the little boat is to the charter. It can serve as a temporary tugboat as you get blown onto the coral or a "funabout" towing the kids on an inflatable tube. But whatever you call it, and however you use it, you need to keep it in good order.

If you need to bail out a lot of rain water from the dinghy you're towing, dip a bucket for the easy bit then pull the plug and drive around on a slight plane until it drains—keeping an eye out for swimmers—and the *Venturi effect* will suck the water out of the drain hole.

When starting the outboard via a pull cord, you can avoid the common problem of bashing people in the head as you pull the cord by ensuring that you are the only person in the dinghy. When you have it running to your satisfaction, invite the rest of the gang to join you.

SOME EASY FIXES FOR COMMON PROBLEMS:

- Before starting, check that the air vent on top of the fuel tank is in the *open* position. If not, the engine will start and run but will quit after about 30 seconds.
- The bulb in the fuel line primes the pump—squeeze the bulb until it feels firm.
- Watch that the fuel line doesn't get pinched by the tank lying on top of it. Or by your foot, for that matter.

If you pull too many times on the outboard's start cord and it fails to start, you may have flooded it with gas/petrol. You can probably smell it too. You'll get it going again if you disconnect the quick-release fuel line from the engine and pull again with the throttle wide open (max revs). It'll likely fire up straight away. Quickly bring down the revs and reconnect the fuel line.

- *Whether you're right or left-handed,* the dinghy is designed for the operator to sit on the starboard-side tube and steer with the left hand because the tiller arm, gear shift and throttle twist rotation are all optimized for this operation.
- Have the person sitting farthest in front hold the painter when underway.
- Don't tie-up too tight to the dock—leave room for others to come in. In a busy area, it's a good idea to leave plenty of painter—a full dinghy length off the dock—so other boaters can fit.
- If you have a choice, tie up on the leeward side of the dinghy dock and if there is any chop or swell running, use the dink's anchor to keep it from smashing against the dock while you're away or—worse—getting crushed beneath it. ALWAYS leave the motor in the *down* position—otherwise you risk having the motor bashed by a moving dink or of damaging someone else's dinghy.
- When operating a charcoal-fired BBQ, keep the dinghy

well clear (if it's in the water) by tying it off to a midships cleat, well forward of the stern.

- Beaching the dinghy is frowned upon by almost every charter company—if not specifically forbidden. Surging swell is too great to risk—even if all is calm when you head off to the restaurant, by the time you get back it could be entirely different. Dinghies can get tossed around, have their anchors torn out or be filled with sand and seawater by just a few unfortunate swells from large power yachts.
- Dinghy painters are one of the most common causes of fouled propellers and drive shafts, so be extra careful when reversing with a dinghy under tow.
- Beach excursions risk bringing sand into the dinghy. Shake off as much as you can before you get in. Once in, trail sandy legs over the side of the dinghy and rinse the sand off. And have a bucket of seawater ready to dip those sandy feet into as soon as you get on the mother ship and before you proceed further. Let no one step off the aft deck until they have thoroughly cleaned their feet and legs.

DINGHY LIGHT. YOUR CHARTER COMPANY SHOULD PROVIDE YOU with the legally required white all-round light. Most don't, but supply a flashlight/torch instead—which is good enough. Make sure that you take it with you when you leave if you're planning on coming back to the boat after sunset. Lots of bareboaters forget when they leave for happy hour in bright sunshine at 1700 and are surprised when it's dark at 1830. As a last resort, turn on your phone and let the light shine outwards. You don't really need the light for illumination—though make sure you don't run over a mooring ball—you need the light so others can see you. And beware of late-night skinny-dippers and other hazards in the busy morning fields!

The Kill Cord: Every dinghy comes equipped with a small plastic clip that slips over a spring-equipped pull-out knob. To start the outboard, this clip must be attached behind the pulled out knob to prevent it from breaking the circuit and stopping the motor from running. This clip is attached to a plastic lanyard **which should be wrapped around the boat operator's wrist,** whenever the motor is running. If the dinghy runs aground, a passenger slips overboard, the boat hits a rock, is swamped by another vessel's wake or any of a number of dangers should occur, the operator has only to jerk her arm to pull out the clip and the motor will instantly stop running. Not everyone does this, since it seems to be an inconvenience but terrible things can happen in a dinghy—particularly where there has been alcohol consumed—not necessarily by the crew on your boat, of course. It's the Caribbean. Rum is involved. Be careful out there.

Chapter 29

DINGHY SECURITY

LIFTING THE DINGHY

On monohulls, there are two circumstances when you'll need to lift your dinghy—or its engine—closer to (or onto) the mothership:

Security: For various reasons—some economic and some just for the pleasure of the thing—your RIB-type dinghy with its 10-15 HP outboard makes a tempting object for thieves. Mostly down-island, but not only there—the rich Virgin Islands have their thieves as well as the less prosperous Grenadines, St. Lucia and Dominica. St. Martin's Grand Case or Marigot bays will sometimes serve as a source of personal transport for Anguillans who have missed the ferry. So, if you're chartering in one of these islands, the briefers at the base will alert you to the risks and guide you on safeguarding your vessel. Recent economic downturns in Puerto Rico and the US Virgins in the aftermath of Hurricanes *Irma* and *Maria* might bode ill for sailors there, too.

THERE ARE TWO MAIN SECURITY SCENARIOS—WHEN THE DINGHY is attached to the mothership whilst all aboard are sleeping, or when the dinghy is at the dock whilst the crew is cavorting—sorry, we mean dining sedately ashore. On the dock, where there are many watching eyes, a basic lock and cable will do—you are really only trying to make your dinghy less attractive a prize than the unlocked one parked right next to it.

When all is quiet in the mooring field and everyone is asleep, using the charter-company supplied wire and padlock often will be insufficient deterrence—the wire alone will not put off experienced thieves. Most will carry a cutter that'll nip through wire before you can say, "Where's the dinghy?" In these places, the charter company will require you to lift your dink up at night before you turn in.

Hang the dinghy off a spare halyard. Lock it, too.

HERE'S HOW:

- Locate the spare halyard, which should be labeled at its rope clutch and tied-off to the base of one of your shrouds. (You can generally identify is as it's usually the only halyard with a shackle end clipped to the mast).

Release the spare halyard from its clutch so you can untie it. This is the line used to lift the dinghy.

- Bring the dink alongside whichever side of the boat the spare halyard is biased toward—which of the side-by-side blocks it enters at the top of the mast. Use the ship's binoculars to check, if need be. On some boats the spare halyard exits at front and center of the mast—in which case either side of the boat will be fine. But do check as, with such a heavy load, you don't want to get your lines crossed.
- With the dinghy alongside and abeam of the gate in the lifelines, release the clutch/line-stopper that's holding it. Move the working end of the spare halyard down to the lifting bridle that, in these theft-prone locations, is generally provided for this purpose. If there is no bridle provided, you can make one with spare dock lines. Attach, with a bowline or the snap-shackle on the end of halyard, to the middle of the bridle.
- Bring the dinghy forward so that the lift point is now abeam of the mast.
- With 4 wraps of the spare halyard around a winch, crank the dink out of the water and about halfway up the side of your boat. Have your crew push the dinghy outwards as it comes up, to lessen any scuffing of the topsides. For extra security, attach the safety cable to the mast or a rail.

SEA CONDITIONS: IN SOME PARTS OF THE CARIBBEAN, PASSAGES cross open, exposed waters. While the sailing can be exhilarating, the dinghy is at risk from being swamped, capsizing or—when going downwind—surfing and overtaking the mothership with a subsequent snap on its painter. To avoid the dink taking such a beating—and, possibly, being lost or damaged—the charter base may request one of two actions:

- Remove the fuel tank and stow it in a cockpit locker—having screwed down the air-vent valve on top of the filler cap. And remount the outboard engine onto the white plastic or wooden pad on the ship's stern (pushpit) railing.
- In addition, they may ask you to lift the dink, with the motor removed, out of the water, over the lifelines and back onto the boat—lashed *upside down* on the foredeck. This is an advanced skill—it won't be necessary on most bareboat charters. If you are planning a long open-water passage, it's a trick worth learning. You'll sail a full knot faster and won't have the noise of the dinghy dragging through your wake for hours on end.

HERE'S HOW:

The motor: Bring the dinghy alongside your boat and secure it as close as you can to the mothership using its painter and a dinghy stern line which, if it's not already attached, you can improvise using any line, such as a dock line. You need to get the dink as close as possible to the sugarscoop stern or fold-down transom. Leave no chance of a gap opening up as you man-handle the engine and other gear out of the dinghy and onto the mothership.

- Most 2-stroke outboard motors are light enough to be lifted by one or two able-bodied persons. If that's not you, or if your boat comes with a heavier 4-stroke motor, bring the dinghy alongside and close to the mast. Use the spare halyard to do the heavy lifting—making sure to tie the halyard to the engine securely.
- Remove the dinghy fuel tank and its quick-connect fuel line from the dink and stow upright—with air vent closed to avoid spillage—in a cockpit locker.
- Remove other loose items like oars and the dinghy anchor and stow them securely. Latch the dinghy's bow

locker if there is one. Carefully rotate the two mounting-bracket screw lugs to allow the motor to be lifted free. The motor will still stay on the transom, even when the lugs are completely undone. But tie a length of light line from a strong point on the motor back to the ship as a safety line, in case the engine should slip or drop during this maneuver.

- With two hands under the strong parts of the motor, front and back but not on the plastic cowling, lift the outboard up and into the dink, with the skeg resting on the hard floor. Keep the engine vertical so it doesn't skid out from you. All the weight will be on the dinghy floor and you're just there to keep it vertical and balanced on its skeg.

- Moving carefully and deliberately, with short steps hop the engine towards the big boat and pass it to a crew member who will receive the engine and hold it, again balanced on its skeg, on the transom step while you get out of the dink.

- Working as a team, move the engine toward the white pad that is fixed to the pushpit/stern railing nearby for the purpose of stowing the motor. Take it easy and don't try to be a hero by lifting any weight that you can't handle fairly easily. Take as many short hops as you need. Lift the engine-mounting bracket up and onto the pad.

- Tighten the mounting screws and use a short length of line to lash the engine to the stern rail or Bimini support to ensure that it doesn't rotate free in waves or when you tack or jibe.

THE DINGHY: LOCATE THE SPARE HALYARD AS ABOVE. YOU'LL USE it to lift the dinghy—this time without the bridle. As above, bring the dink alongside whichever side of the boat the spare halyard is biased toward where it enters the top part of the mast.

- With the dinghy alongside and abeam of the gate in the lifelines, have one of your crew release the clutch/line-stopper that's holding it and take the bitter end of the spare halyard down to the metal U-bolt or whatever the painter is attached to. As you lean forward over the bow of the dinghy, the U-bolt may be a little below the waterline.
- You don't need to tie a knot below water—just pass the line through the metal fitting and bring it back to a comfortable height above water in front of you. Now you'll need to tie a bowline.
- Have the person in the dinghy clamber out onto the mothership and grind the spare halyard winch.
- Big bareboats have big RIB-style dinks these days. They are heavy. If you have a power winch, it'll drain your batteries lifting the thing. Fire up your engine and run at around 2000 rpm in neutral as you lift. If there's no power winch, get the strongest crew members to take turns grinding the manual winch.
- As the nose of the dink comes out of the water, position somone to grab the bow of the dink forward of the mast and push it outwards to avoid scuffing the topsides.
- Raise it so the back ends of the tubes just slide over the lifelines and maneuver it toward the big boat's centerline. You'll need to release the headsail sheet on the side that you're lifting—making sure that the sheet is not trapped beneath or otherwise impeded after the dink is lashed down.
- Twist the dink so, as the spare halyard is eased, it falls slowly *upside down* on the big boat's centerline, with the dinghy transom close to the front of the mast to create space forward and provide a buffer if you encounter blue water coming over the deck.

- Release the halyard and use any available line (including the painter) to thoroughly lash down the little boat to the big one. Make it hold fast. The *trucker's hitch* is a good one for this job.
- Job done. Award whoever cranked-up the dink an extra ration of rum—or icecream—to be received once you've reached your next destination safely.

Chapter 30

PLUG'N'PLAY

POWER POINTS

The electrical conveniences made possible by the generator on modern boats have made massive and welcome improvements to the quality of life aboard ship. Aircon! Microwave! Big-Screen Video! Watermaker! All amazing. And the increases in power requirements for the old familiar chart plotters, ice makers and other devices have made the genny the go-to source for battery charging, too. But often these sophisticated displays and devices are treated with a casual disregard rather than the molly-coddling they deserve—and, frankly, require.

Marine electronics are just as sensitive as those you have at home. You wouldn't dream of just pulling the plug on your appliances lest you destroy the careful programming you've entered. Same with that color chart plotter for instance: it's a computer, with sensitivities to match. Ditto with the other navigation instruments, air conditioning units, refrigeration and entertainment equipment. Plus, they live near salt water, and other indignities such as spilled drinks.

When first boarding the charter yacht, or when receiving the Boat Briefing, look in the chart table or under the seat nearby for a copy of the electronics manuals. Spend a few minutes learning the basics of how the chartplotter and VHF operate. If the manual has been removed or can't be found, you can easily look the model up on the internet. You need to know how to properly start them up and how to manage the waypoints and routes that have most likely been installed by previous operators. Ignore all waypoints and routes since you can't be sure of their accuracy—delete them if you have the time. Learn the proper procedure for powering up all instruments. When it comes to powering-down these devices, remember to turn off the individual power buttons at each instrument at the helm station. Don't just flick the breaker at the electrical panel.

Air conditioning is the big game-changing application on the modern cruising yacht. It does require some special handling, though. If you're on a boat with a generator, the air conditioning units need to be turned off at the individual cabin controls before disconnecting from shore power. The reason to turn them on and off individually and not via the main breaker is that, if left on, when the generator is fired up and the aircon breaker flipped on there's such a huge current draw when 2-3 units start at the same time that the generator will likely shut itself down in protest. They need to be powered up one-by-one with a 5-10 minute delay between each.

Monohull charter yachts may have the generator positioned between the two aft cabins or in a dedicated space in the cockpit and the A/C distributed in three zones—Forward cabin(s), Saloon, and Aft cabins. The reality of onboard air conditioning is that it is not easy to maintain a temperature—it's often bone-chillingly cold or barely cool. Make sure you get plenty of blankets at the start of the journey to compensate for the chill.

NOTE: In your cabins, keep the sun-shields closed under your hatches and the blinds closed to prevent them becoming green-houses during the day. It'll be a lot easier and quicker for the genset to cool them down at the end of the day.

Also don't unplug your boat from shore power without first powering down all the heavy energy consumers on your boat, starting with all the aircon units at the individual saloon and cabin controls and *then* all the 110/220 volt aircon and battery charger breakers at the nav. station followed by turning off the 110/220 volt AC input breaker or change-over gate. Only then unplug from the power post —after turning that off, too—you don't want any risk of a current arc.

State of Charge: During your first 24 hours aboard, pay special attention to electrical consumption as displayed at the breaker panel. Not all battery systems on charter yachts are maintained to perfection, so you'll need to make sure your batteries hold sufficient charge to chill the refrigerators overnight.

A fully charged 12-volt battery system should be taken to a level of 14.2-14.4 volts initially, if there is no drain on the system. Once the charger is disconnected, the voltage should fall to around 12.8 volts. If the batteries don't reach that level after hours of charging, or if they rapidly lose their charge, you may have problems.

Not only will you have smelly fish in the fridge but the low-voltage alarm will probably kick in around 2am, disturbing your slumber. A battery system with a level of 12 volts will have lost 75% of its charge and needs to be reconnected to the charger.

If you run the generator all night, then batteries should be well charged, provided you have switched on the *breaker for the battery charger*!

Associated with all this charging capacity is the necessity, once the generator and engines are off, to conserve the voltage you've created. Turn off any fans or lights when you're not in the cabin. Monitor the CD player and other electronics—are they burbling away in a part of the boat where no one can hear them?

As part of the daily routine, check the status of the batteries from the saloon control panel. If the voltage is below 12v, you'll need to run the engine or the generator to charge up again if you want things to keep working.

And be aware that the recommendation for most charter yachts is that the generator not be running whilst the vessel is underway.

The reason being that the water intake for the genny is close to the surface and can easily suck in seaweed and other substances as the boat rolls in swell or when beating upwind. Clearing that mess is a big job and best avoided by not incurring the problem in the first place.

Chapter 31

CHECKS AND BALANCES

Daily Practice

WOPILG

Water Out:

- Close port lights and hatches tight.
- Pump bilges.

People In:

- Remind everyone it's a boat, not a holiday cottage.
- "One hand for me and one for the ship."
- Close all the gates at the side and back of the boat.

Look Good:

- Laundry off the lifelines.
- Swim ladder up.
- All doors, lockers, drawers, fridges, oven doors, secured

from slamming about when underway.

WOBBLE

W *Water filter*: Check for debris.

O *Oil levels*: Check the dipstick for quantity and color.

B *Belts*: Check tightness and degree of wear.

B *Bilge*: look beneath the engine for leaks.

L *Look Around:* Check engine compartment for loose filler caps, nuts and bolts etc.

E *Engine/Exhaust:* Look for lines in the water. After starting engine look for cooling water exiting the exhaust.

LOCK, LASH AND SECURE

When preparing for departure, look around above and below decks, checking for weak points in these areas:

Hatches and ports: The hatches and opening portlights (aka 'windows') should already be closed but now's the time to double-check that they've been closed securely. Pay extra attention to the more common Lewmar hatches, which are sometimes on a half-latch that looks secure but which is not watertight (it's designed to allow some ventilation whilst keeping rain out.)

Dinghy: If you're sailing a monuhull and towing the little boat, lengthen the tow to the painter's maximum length once you're clear of the marina or anchorage/mooring field. (If wind and sea conditions are boisterous, rig up a Y-shaped towing bridle from a dock line and attach an end to a cleat on either side of the hull). Bring the fuel tank aboard the big boat and secure it upright in a cockpit locker—put a couple of fenders temporarily in an aft cabin if you need space. When getting under way, experiment with the towline length until you get the dink positioned just right. If necessary, tie together a couple of docklines so the dinghy can be towed at a distance behind the charter yacht—particularly if there's some swell.

Doors, Drawers, Lockers, and Cabinets: These should already be locked if you're sailing. Before a squall hits your boat, make sure that doors and drawers can't fly open, throwing their contents into the boat or at whoever may be down below. Pay special attention to drawers with knives and lockers containing glass jars and wine bottles. You do not want to be cleaning up spilled olive oil, soy sauce, and ketchup in a rocking boat.

We often find that the common push-button locks on bare boats don't engage or properly secure their drawer. If this is the case, use some surgical tape from the First Aid kit to temporarily do the job. Tell the charter company afterward so they can both fix the lock and top up the First Aid kit.

Better yet, bring a roll of strong masking (not duct) tape to secure drawers, oven door (if it doesn't have its own dedicated lock) and the like. If you do leave some marks when removing tape, try spraying mosquito repellent on the mess and rubbing with a strong cloth. This stuff will take Sharpie marks off fiberglass tables and other places, too.

One friend described being in a storm en route to Panama. She was doing OK until "the stove came out of its gimbals and flew across the cabin right at me." The trip of a lifetime lasted until they got to the Canal entrance, when she flew home. Keep everything secure!

Keep any water-sensitive items like smartphones and cameras in a dry bag or even a Zip-lock style disposable. But if you have a Go Pro, clamp it on somewhere, point it at the helm and turn it on. You are bound to get some great footage!

Heads and showers: Drain all toilet bowls of as much water as possible and lower the lid—objects can fall into the bowl easily in bouncy seas. Drain the shower sump also, since there are often a few cups of gray water sluicing around. Secure toothbrushes, shampoo, and glass items, towels and anything that might fall and get wet or break.

Breaker panel: Turn off power to all units that don't need to be on. Lights, fans, and air conditioning units—and any other extraneous electrical equipment. Do leave the bilge pumps on, though, since the movement will send trapped water sloshing about the bilges to trip the float switches.

Chapter 32

FEELING WOOZY

SEASICKNESS

Nothing will impact your happiness aboard the yacht as much as a case of *mal de mer*. Not only your happiness, should you be the one suffering, but the happiness of those around you. If you know or suspect that you or anyone aboard is susceptible, then it is essential you take adequate *preventative* action.

There are a number of medications available for seasickness but they each have their complications. Many of these remedies will induce drowsiness, lethargy, dry mouth, and other symptoms. The most important part of taking these meds is to *take them early*. Most are for prevention of sea-sickness, not its cure. If you feel symptoms, it is often too late to do anything.

The most effective drug seems to be the Scopolamine transdermal patch. Talk to your doctor first—there may be side effects that won't help your situation. For most people though, this is amazingly effective and has minimal side effects. Every other remedy pales in comparison.

The other common medication is Stugeron—which is frowned upon by the US Food and Drug Administration but widely accepted in Europe, the UK, and elsewhere. You may be able to buy it over the counter in some island jurisdictions

For those with occasionally mild reactions, ginger can work wonders. Crystallized ginger is good or ginger in various candy or chewable forms. Straight ginger root is good, too—grate some fresh ginger into soda water or add the ginger to a cup of tea. Some of the fizzy soft drinks like ginger beer can be a good stomach settler— but make sure your choice contains actual ginger and not just a ginger flavoring.

Duty requires we point out that sea-sickness is associated with hangovers and alcohol—it might be best to refrain from excessive indulgence! One side effect of drinking alcohol, of course, is dehydration. Stay hydrated.

If a member of your party does come down with the Queazies, get them into the water when you're anchored or moored. A lot of the problem lies in the confusion induced by the rapid movements in all three dimensions as the yacht is rocked by swell and wind. If you are able to stop in a cove and get the crew swimming, the mood generally improves immensely.

If all else fails, ease the ailing mariner into the shade of a palm tree and let them regain their equilibrium—minus the Painkiller.

GLOSSARY

A.

Aback. The condition of a sail when trimmed to windward.

Abaft. Nearer the stern.

Abeam. At right angles to the middle of the boat.

Aboard. On the boat.

Adrift. Not under power or sail, not anchored or moored. Drifting.

Aft and After. Direction. Back or behind. The aft deck. Go aft to the stern.

Aground. Insufficient flotation. Stuck to the seabed. Caught in coral.

Ahead. In front of the boat.

Aloft. Up the mast or rigging. High above deck.

Amidships. In the middle part of the vessel.

Anchor. Equipment deployed from the vessel to secure it to the seabed. Usually heavy metal with pointed ends to dig into the bottom. May be used at bow or stern.

Anchor light. 360 degree visible white light signifying the vessel is at anchor. To be shown between sunset and sunrise. Usually at top of mast.

Anchor watch. Deployment of crew to observe that vessel holds position while at anchor.

Angle of attack. Angle between the sail chord line (imaginary line drawn between luff and leech of the sail) and the apparent wind.

Anticipatory steering. When sailing downwind the following sea sometimes will lift the stern and turn the boat, changing the wind angle. It is often necessary to turn the boat before this happens, or just as it happens, to avoid an accidental jibe.

Apparent wind. The combination of the True or Actual wind and the wind created by the vessel's movement, as experienced aboard ship.

Arc of turn. the arc described by the vessel's *pivot point* during a turn.

Autopilot. Automatic steering controlled by GPS or other technology.

Aweigh. Raising the anchor from the seabed. Feeling the weight of the anchor.

B

Back. To trim the sail to the windward side. Usually the foresail but could be the main also. Secondary: wind shifting counter-clockwise.

Backstay. A stay supporting the mast from the stern of the boat.

Balance. Relationship of power created by forward and aft sails.

Batten. A rod or strip, often fiberglass, used to stiffen the leech of a sail.

Batten pocket. A shape sewn in to the sail that holds the batten.

Beam. The widest part of the boat

Beam reach. Point of sail with apparent wind coming over the beam

Bear away. To turn away from the wind. Aka: Fall off.

Bearing. The angle an object lies in relation to the boat expressed in degrees.

Beat. Sailing close hauled.

Below. Beneath the deck. At the bottom of the companionway.

Berth. A sailor's bed. ALSO A vessel's allotted space at dock or slip.

Bight. A loop in a line.

Bimini. Canvas cover often supported by a tubed frame to create shade and shelter in the cockpit.

Binnacle. A support and enclosure for a compass.

Bitter end. The loose end of a line. See *working end.*

Block. A device used to change the angle of a line; a pulley.

Board. To go on a boat; as in: Let's board the boat now.

Boat Boy. Person offering services in an anchorage or mooring field.

Boat hook. Pole with a hook to lift and handle line.

Bollard. A short post on a dock to which a mooring line is attached.

Boom. A spar that supports the foot of the mainsail.

Boom vang. A device to hold the boom down or to prevent from rising.

Bow. The forward part of a boat. Also called 'the pointy end'.

Bow pulpit. Guardrail and support at the bow for the lifelines.

Bow line. A dock line used to secure the bow to a dock.

Bowline. Non-slipping temporary loop knot.

Breast line. Dock line leading abeam from midships to a cleat or bollard

Bridgedeck. The deck that joins the hulls on a catamaran.

Bridgedeck slam. Sound and vibration resulting from swell hitting the bridgedeck, usually when sailing or motoring upwind.

Bridle. A line used to distribute the load from a tow or an anchor to two points on the boat.

Broach. To be overpowered to the point that the boat becomes unbalanced and the vessel tends to round up into the wind.

Broad reach. Point of sail with the wind coming over the boat's quarter.

Bulkhead. A support, at right angles to the centerline below deck, to strengthen the boat.

By the lee. Sailing on a run with the wind coming over the same side of the boat as the boom is on. Sometimes a precursor to an accidental jibe.

C

Cabin. A room in a boat.

Calm. No movement of wind.

Capsize. Overturned in the water.

Cardinal points. North, South, East, and West.

Cast off. To let go a line, usually a dock line.

Catamaran. Vessel with 2 equal-sized hulls in parallel.

Cay. Low-lying island of sand or coral. (Pron. "Key")

Center of effort. The point in a sail where the effects of all wind forces come to a focus.

Center of lateral resistance. The point where all forces on underwater appendages (hull, rudder, keel) come to a focus.

Chafe. Repetitive wearing by friction on a line or sheet.

Chain plate. Metal fitting by which stays attach to the hull.

Channel. A navigable stretch of water usually defined by landforms (islands), buoys, or markers.

Chart. A nautical map showing depths and features both underwater and on land.

Charter. Contractual renting of a vessel for pleasure or trade.

Chop. Short and steep wave action. Sometimes associated with action of wind against tide.

Cleat. A two-horned fitting on the boat or on a dock for attaching a mooring line.

Cleat hitch. Knot used to attach dockline to a cleat.

Clew. The lower aft point of a sail.

Close-hauled. Point of sail allowing the vessel to sail as close to the wind direction as possible.

Close reach. Point of sail several degrees off the wind from the close haul.

Clove hitch. Temporary hitch used to attach e.g.fenders to a lifeline or rail.

Cockpit. Part of the deck that accommodates crew when sailing the boat.

Cockpit locker. Storage areas located beneath seating in the cockpit.

Code flags. See 'signal flags'.

Coil. Circular arrangement of line for storage.

COLREGS. The International Regulations for Preventing Collisions at Sea. AKA The Rules of the Road.

Companionway. Steps leading from cockpit to interior of the yacht, usually a monohull.

Compass. A magnetically sensitive instrument that points to magnetic North and displays Cardinal Points and degrees.

Compass card. Disk in the center of the compass with all points and degrees printed upon it.

Course. The heading or direction the boat is steered.

Crew. Persons involved in operating the vessel.

Cringle. A reinforced eye in the sail with a metal insert to accept a line.

Cruising boat. A boat designed for comfort more than speed. Not primarily a race boat.

Current. Horizontal movement of water resulting largely from action of wind or tide.

D

Dead. Precisely. Dead ahead.

Dead in the water. Not making way. Without power.

Dead reckoning. A method of calculating current position from the heading, speed and time from a known point. Derived from Deduced Reckoning.

Deck. Topmost horizontal surface of the vessel.

Depower. To reduce the effectiveness of sails, usually to reduce heeling.

Depth sounder. Electronic device to measure depth of the water.

Dinghy. The small boat used to convey passengers ashore and for myriad duties.

Distance off. How far the boat is from a point of land, dock, or mooring, as measured by a crew member.

Dock. The shore-side structure the boat can tie up to.

Dock line. A line used to attach a boat to a dock, often made from nylon.

Dodger. A spray shield that protects the cockpit from rain and spray. Can often be folded out of the way.

Douse. To furl or drop a sail.

Downwind. The direction towards which the wind is flowing.

Draft. The vertical depth of the hull and keel. OR the depth of the curved sail.

Drag. Anchor not firmly attached to the bottom, pulling free.

Drift. The measurement of the speed of a current.

E

Ease. To reduce tension on a sheet or line.

Ebb. Decrease in the height of the tide. The associated current is the ebb current.

Emergency tiller. An auxiliary tiller designed to fit the top of the rudder post—usually when steering cables fail.

Eye of the wind. Pointed directly into the wind.

F

Fair. Without obstruction. A running line must be led fair.

Fairlead. A fitting to direct a line, reduce chafe, clear an obstruction etc.

Fairway. The deep, navigable part of a channel.

Fake. Laying large loops of line to avoid tangles.

Fall off. To turn away from the wind.

Falls. Block and tackle fittings for raising and lowering dinghy.

Feathering. Sailing deliberately too high to slow the boat.

Fend off. To push away, to avoid by pushing when too close to another vessel or obstacle etc.

Fender. Inflatable or shock absorbing device to protect the vessel from scrapes, as in docking.

Figure eight. A stopper knot, used to add bulk to the end of a line so as to prevent it slipping through a chock.

Fix. A known, verified position.

Flake. Variant of *Fake* (see above).

Flood. Current creating a rising tide.

Fluky. Winds that are light and variable.

Following sea. Waves coming from behind the vessel.

Foot. the bottom edge of a sail.

Foot off. To turn the vessel slightly away from the wind when sailing close hauled in order to gain speed.

Foresail. Sail that is forward of the mast.

Forestay. Stay supporting the mast from the bow of the boat. It may be attached lower than the top of the mast.

Foretriangle. The area defined by the mast, deck, and forestay.

Forward. Toward the bow.

Foul. Tangled or kinked with reference to a line or rode. OR The condition of the seabed.

Freeboard. The distance from the deck to the waterline.

Full sail. When all sail is set. Without reefs.

Furl. To douse a sail still attached to a spar or mandrel.

Furling line. Dedicated line for furling sail on a roller system.

G.

Galley. The kitchen on a boat.

Genoa. A large foresail. The clew extends beyond the foretriangle.

Gimbal. Swinging supports that allow a stove, compass etc. to stay level while boat is in motion.

Give-way vessel. The vessel that must keep out of the way of another vessel.

Glide zone. The distance a moving vessel will continue to move once power is taken off.

Gooseneck. The fitting that attaches the boom to the mast.

Grommet. A small snap ring sewn into canvas.

Ground tackle. The anchor and anchor rode, including swivels and attachments..

Gust. A strong puff of wind.

H

Halyard. A line dedicated to raising a sail.

Hard over. The helm turned as far as possible

Hatch. Securable opening in the deck.

Head. Top corner of a triangular sail. OR A bathroom on a boat. OR, The front area of the boat.

Head down. To turn away from the wind. To fall off.

Head to wind. Pointing the boat directly into the eye of the wind.

Head up. To turn closer to the wind

Header. When sailing upwind, a shift in wind direction or speed requiring a turn away from the wind.

Heading. The course to steer.

Headsail. A foresail.

Headstay. A forestay that runs from the bow to the top of the mast.

Heave. To throw a line.

Heave to. A technique to safely stop the boat's motion while under sail.

Heavy weather. Strong wind and large waves.

Heel. The tilting or tipping angle the boat sails at.

High. Sailing high is to sail less efficiently by being closer to the wind than optimal.

Hitch. A type of knot that is tied around or to an object, such as a cleat.

Holding ground. The type of bottom in an anchorage.

Hull. The underbody of a boat..

Hover. To maintain a static position when waiting for another vessel to move off a dock or mooring, or in other close-quarters situation.

In irons. Head to wind and not moving through the water.

Inboard. Inside the boat.

J

Jackline or safety line. A line or strap on deck running fore and aft upon which safety harnesses can be tethered

Jib. A foresail that fits inside the foretriangle.

Jib sheet. A line that controls the horizontal movement of the jib.

Jibe. To turn the stern of the boat through the eye of the wind.

K

Kedge anchor. Any anchor used to kedge off.

Kedge off. Using an anchor to pull the boat into deeper water.

Keel. On monohulls, an attachment to the hull, usually lead or cast iron, that provides weight for stability, and increases lateral resistance. On catamarans, the keels are lightweight and provide lateral resistance and protection for the hulls.

Knot. A fastening made by tying ends of line together.

L

Lash. Tie down.

Lazy jacks. Lines running between the boom and mast that prevent the mainsail from falling on deck when reefing or dropping sail.

Lazy sheet. The sheet not under tension, the windward sheet (usually).

Lee and leeward (pronounced "lee" and "loo-ward"). Downwind, in relation to a reference point. "The anchorage is sheltered in the lee of the island."

Leeward boat. When two boats are on the same tack the windward boat shall keep out of the way of the leeward boat

Lee shore. The shore that is to leeward of the boat.

Lifeline. A wire or cable that runs around the perimeter of the deck and is supported by stanchions.

Lift. Opposite of header, a wind shift allowing the helmsperson, when sailing upwind, to steer closer to the desired course.

Lift point. The point at which the weight of anchor rode lifts from the seabed. In calm conditions this point is close to the vessel but in windy conditions is closer to the anchor.

Line of approach. Course derived from a *transit* that leads vessel to a desired point.

Luff. The leading edge of a sail, OR the flapping of a sail when poorly trimmed or too close to the wind.

M

Mandrel. A vertical metallic rod to which a sail is attached and around which it is spun when furling.

Marina. An arrangement of docks providing spaces for boats to tie up.

Mediterranean (Med.) mooring. Lying to the shore or dock with the bow held by an anchor and the stern tied off to the shore or dock.

Minimal control speed (MCS). When motoring, the least amount of speed required to keep water flowing over the rudder(s). Often achieved by pulsing the shifter in and out of gear and allowing the boat to glide before re-engaging transmission.

Mooring. A permanent anchor with an attached floating buoy.

N

Nautical mile. One minute of latitude or about 1.15 statute miles.

Neap tide. The weaker tides that occur during quarter phases of the moon.

O

On the slip. To tie the tail of a line as a loop to make untying a knot easier.

Operatic method. A way of throwing a line around a mooring ball or dock cleat/bollard. Both arms are flung wide as the line is released but the bitter end is grasped, securing the line in a loop.

Outboard. Outside the hull OR A removable engine for dinghy.

Outhaul. A line fixed to the clew of the mainsail for tensioning its foot.

Overpowered. Too much power in the sails producing excessive heel and difficult steering.

Override. When a wrap of line runs over another wrap on a winch.

P

Painter. The line attached to the bow of a dinghy.

Pay out. To ease or surge a line.

Piloting. The art of navigating by eye in coastal waters.

Pinch. Inadvertently sailing too close to the wind—not to be confused with *feathering.*

Pivot point. The point around which the vessel turns. If travelling forward, the point moves towards the bow and when traveling astern, the point moves aft.

Pre-emptive steering. See *anticipatory steering.*

Prop walk. The tendency of a propeller turning in reverse to pull the stern of a monohull vessel sideways when making way.

Prop wash. By giving a short burst of power, the propeller creates a wash of turbulent water that hits the turned rudder and pushes the stern of the vessel sideways

Pulpit. A metal railing at the stern and/or bow that serves to support nav. lights, lifelines etc.

Pushpit. Britishism for Stern Rail.

Q

Quarter. The area between the beam and stern.

Quay. A dock, often of solid stone, open on both sides.

R

Radar reflector. Device fixed to the mast or attached to the rigging that reflects radar waves.

Ready about. A command issued prior to tacking; as in: Ready about...Tacking.

Reef. To reduce sail area OR a shoal area of sand, rock or coral.

Rig. The mast, boom, and stays.

Right of way. A way of describing the provisions of COLREGS, which spell out the rights and responsibilities between approaching vessels.

Roach. Large expanse of sail on the leech of the mainsail extending aft of an imaginary line from the top of the mast to the end of the boom.

Rode. The anchor cable including chain and rope.

Rolling hitch. A very important knot used to tie one line to another in order to reduce the strain or to act as a snubber, create a bridle etc.

Round turn and two half hitches. A type of knot that constricts with more tension in the line.

Running. A point of sail deep downwind.

Running lights. The lights a boat shows at night.

Running rigging. All the moveable lines that control any part of the sails or other equipment, such as a spinnaker pole.

S.

Safety net. The net in the bow area of a catamaran sometimes called the trampoline.

Safety netting. Netting attached to the lifelines to protect young children from falling overboard.

Sail drive. Propulsion method where propeller is directly beneath engine and attached by a z-shaped drive shaft.

Saloon. The large common dining and social area below deck on a boat.

Sea room. The distance between the boat and shore.

Seacock. A valve to shut off flow from a through-hull fitting.

Secure. To fasten to a dock or cleat.

Set. The direction in which a current is traveling.

Shackle. A metal device that secures a line to another object.

Sheave. The round turning part in a block or pulley.

Sheet bend. A type of knot used to tie together two lines of unequal diameter.

Shoal. A shallow area of rock or coral.

Shroud. On monohulls, side support wires, or sometimes rods, fastened to chainplates in the hull holding the mast upright in column and supporting it laterally. On catamarans they are led further aft and also support the mast fore-and-aft in a tripod arrangement with the forestay. Located close to midships. Generally stainless steel.

Skeg. A small appendage on the hull near the stern

Skipper. The person who is in charge

Slip. A berth in a marina.

Snub. Wrapping a line around a cleat or winch to reduce the load while still maintaining control of the line.

Snubber. A line that takes the strain off the anchor chain and acts as a shock absorber.

Sole. The cabin floor.

Spring line. A line led forward or aft on a vessel. Used when docked to control its fore and aft motion. Each line is named for its point of attachment to the boat and the direction it travels towards the dock, eg. Midships aft spring.

Spring tide. The more powerful tide at the new and full moon.

Stability. Resistance to heeling.

Stand-on vessel. The vessel that is obliged to maintain course and speed in a crossing situation.

Standing rigging. All wires or cables that hold up the mast.

Stay. A wire or cable supporting the mast.

Steerageway. Having enough speed through the water to steer the boat.

Stern line. A dock line that secures the stern from sideways motion.

Stern rail. Guardrail and support for the lifelines at the stern of the boat.

Sternway. Moving backwards through the water.

Stiffness. Resistance to heeling.

Stow. To put items away on a boat.

SUP. Stand-up paddleboard.

Surf. To glide/slide down the face of a wave.

T

Tack. The foremost, lower point of a sail.

Tail. Pulling on a line after it leaves the winch to increase the grip of the winch.

Thimble. A metal or plastic ring inside an eye splice that protects the line from chafe.

Through-hull fitting. A metal or plastic fitting providing a secure attachment point to allow the transfer of fluids through the hull of the boat.

Topping lift. A line led, often from the deck through a sheave at the top of the mast, to the end of the boom to support it when no sail is hoisted.

Topsides. The hull area between waterline and deck.

Trucker's hitch. A type of knot used like a block and tackle to increase the amount of tension in a line

True wind. The wind velocity and direction as felt were the boat not moving.

U

Under power. With the engine running and in gear. Sails may be up or down.

Underway. Making way through the water.

V

Vang. A block-and-tackle system for exerting downward pressure on the boom. Also (British) known as a kicking strap or kicker.

Veer. A clockwise shift of the wind.

Velocity shift. When the change of wind speed produces a directional change in the apparent wind.

Venturi effect. The result of a fluid (such as water) being forced through a small diameter hole. Pressure decreases and velocity increases. Often used to clear water from a flooded dinghy etc.

VHF. Very high frequency radio used onboard for communications.

VMG. Velocity Made Good. Speed of approach towards your desired destination as compared with velocity through the water or over the ground.

W *Watch.* Those crew on deck and responsible for the safe operation of the boat

Way and Making way. Motion through the water

Weather helm. The tendency of a boat to turn towards the wind.

Weather vane. 1) noun: device atop the mast to indicate wind direction; 2) verb: tendency of the boat to point into the wind when the mainsail only is deployed. Weather helm.

Windage. The effect of the wind on exposed surfaces of the vessel. More pronounced on a catamaran than a monohull.

Windlass. Winch for the anchor rode.

Windward. Towards the wind, upwind.

Windward boat. The boat that is further upwind.

LINKS

Contact us at: info@smartercharterguides.com

On Facebook: facebook.com/CharterGuides/

On the Web: smartercharterguides.com

All links mentioned in this text are accessible from the web site at https://wp.me/P9jJzL-53

Acknowledgments

The authors wish to thank the hundreds of students, clients, and colleagues who have been the catalysts for this project. Without their questions, comments, and enthusiastic commitment to the art and science of cruising under sail, we wouldn't have started down this path.

We would also like to thank the management and ownership of the many charter companies who have encouraged us in putting these books together.

Special thanks to Kim Downing for the excellent illustrations.

A NOTE ON THE AUTHORS:

Neither of us started out in a sailing school. While we may have put together a number of instructor credentials and professional qualifications, our sailing was mostly learned piecemeal—some from friends, from dads, some from Scouts, some from friends, and a good deal from racing. Much of this was of great value and some—such as racing—less so.

(We don't wish to demean yacht racing, but it is by definition the very epitome of imprudent seamanship—where you learn to carry too much sail for too long in too much wind—but lots of fun both on and off the water).

We've been sailing Caribbean waters for decades, in many capacities—from sailing instructor to charter company owner, corporate manager, and professional coach. Between us we've seen it all and done most of it. We've made mistakes, dragged anchor, snagged propellers, bounced off docks and off the seabed—so we know what we are talking about. *"If you haven't been aground, you haven't been around,"* they say. Well, we've been around.

Michael sailed in America's Cup-level competition in the 1983 British challenger, *Victory*. David pottered around on boats in New Zealand and Australia. We both taught sailing on New York harbor at the same time—without knowing each other, though we did wave hello as we sailed by—under the shadow of the Twin Towers. And we survived the tugboats, cruise ships, freighters, garbage scows, Thursday night racers, as well as day-tripping tour boats. That experience led us here to save you from many of the mistakes and misfortunes that have come our way. And to share the joys and satisfactions, too.

Things have changed in the Caribbean this year, at least our part of it. And the future is a little less predictable than we thought it was just a few months ago–a fact that might make these books even more useful than we had imagined. But we are betting that the waters will soon be blessed with yachts under sail and sailors overjoyed. We intend to be among them and hope you'll be there too.

Michael (L) and David (R) snapping a selfie outside the Royal BVI Yacht Club. Taking the salute is Michael's son, James.

Contact: info@smartercharterguides.com